MAXIMIZING MINICOURSES

A Practical Guide to a Curriculum Alternative

Albert I. Oliver

TEACHERS COLLEGE PRESS
Teachers College, Columbia University
New York, New York

Library of Congress Cataloging in Publication Data

Oliver, Albert I
    Maximizing minicourses.

    (Practical suggestions for teaching series)
    Includes bibliographical references.
    1. Curriculum enrichment. I. Title. II. Series:
Practical suggestions for teaching.
LB1570.052   375'.001   77-13942
ISBN 0-8077-2520-X

FIRST PRINTING

Printed in the United States of America

To the many schools across the nation
who shared their hopes, their
struggles, their successes.

INTRODUCTION

Since the 1960's, there have been calls from many sources for greater "relevance" in curriculum. A number of commission and panel reports urging reform in secondary education have advocated that students be provided with a variety of educational options and alternative programs both within and outside the school as a means of achieving increased relevance. The Kettering Commission's *Task Force '74* suggested consideration of alternatives under two broad headings: one which includes the degree of structure, including the use of space allocation and allocation of time; the other which includes curricular design and the student population served. An earlier Kettering Commission panel suggested that the variety of alternatives available to students should be "limited only by the legitimate needs of adolescents and the vivacity and imagination of educational planners." The minicourse concept—courses that are short-term and elective—represents one of the variety of educational options which can be made available for learners.

Professor Albert Oliver, an experienced practitioner and theorist in curriculum improvement, has written a concise yet comprehensive book on minicourses—what they are, what purposes they can serve, how one goes about developing minicourses at various school levels (elementary, middle, and secondary), and how one evaluates such experiences. This book was developed as a result of Oliver's extensive visits to schools across the nation where minicourses of various kinds were being offered. In dozens of settings, Oliver observed minicourses in action; talked with students, teachers, and administrators about such experiences; and gathered data from which he developed the insights he shares with readers. In addition to on-site visits, Oliver collected descriptive material about minicourses from more than 300 schools throughout the United States.

This book provides the reader with practical, detailed, useful information about minicourses. The information and suggestions will enable persons implementing the minicourse concept in their own schools to design and effect such learning opportunities. The book presents a good mix of theory and practice so that readers will understand the theoretical basis for the practical suggestions offered.

> — A. Harry Passow
> Jacob H. Schiff Professor of Education
> Teachers College, Columbia University

AUTHOR'S PREFACE

Options? Alternatives? Electives? Short term? These are some of the questions that are being raised concerning ways to vitalize the curriculum. The pages that follow look at principles, practices, and problems associated with a concept called the "minicourse."

The material for this book has been drawn from the ideas and actual experiences of schools and schools systems throughout the United States. The data were gathered by writing to school systems across the country. These reports were supplemented with personal visits to a variety of schools and an extensive review of the literature—especially educational periodicals—dealing with the topic. The result is a sampling of actual school practices from Maine to Hawaii and Florida to Alaska with many stops in between. As a result, on hand are letters, reports, school catalogues, and memoranda from over 300 schools. These, then, form the background for this book.

From an analysis made of the material, plus observations and many discussions with administrators, department chairmen, teachers, students, and parents, certain questions and problems emerged. These form the basis for the chapters that follow. Practical answers to questions raised by experience are presented along with actual examples from the field that show both reality and variation.

Tying the samplings together offers a look at theoretical bases upon which curriculum alternatives may be built. It is interesting to note that a study of options should find so many options.

This book should be helpful to anyone looking for ideas-in-action: prospective teachers, classes in curriculum development, administrators and teachers involved in staff development, curriculum committees, and interested laymen. A list of selected references for those who wish to explore some ideas further follows each chapter.

> — Albert I. Oliver
> University of Pennsylvania

CONTENTS

MAXIMIZING MINICOURSES

Chapter 1

WHY MAKE A MINI?

The intent of a mobile curriculum is to shift the respon-
sibility for learning from the school to the student.
—Curriculum Office Motto,
Urbandale High School, Iowa

One might observe that a curriculum theorist is one who is always looking into the distant skies. A curriculum practioner, on the other hand, is more concerned with realities down on the ground. Once in a while he or she looks up when the word gets around that there is a new light in the sky. Will it be a guiding light or just a flashy meteor that soon will burn out? Now and then the theorist and the practitioner become a pair of curriculum stargazers as they mutually find excitement in a new star and wonder what it portends. Can they get a fix on it and thus plot their own course? In the 1960s a new curriculum "star" appeared on the educational horizon—the minicourse. What was there in this phenomenon that drew and then held both the theorist and the program planner in the school? The following pages will attempt to answer this question by looking at both the motives advanced and the courses produced by school leaders who "hitched their wagons" to the minicourse.

Purposes the Minicourse Can Serve

An examination of the documents put out by school systems offering minicourses reveals an interesting array of purposes. An analysis (based on a nation-wide sampling by the author) of statements and descriptive material about minicourses from over 300 schools throughout the United States indicates as many as 50

3

different goals which they hoped to attain through the installation of these programs. Of these goals, the ones most frequently mentioned were:

- Involving the learner in program planning and implementation.
- Capitalizing upon the interests of the learner.
- Utilizing the interests and strengths of the teachers.
- Improving teaching.
- Increasing the scope of the curriculum.
- Providing a more relevant educational program.
- Developing student responsibility.
- Providing students with options.
- Tying the community and the school closer together.
- Providing an opportunity to experiment with course offerings.

In the pages that follow, there will be a discussion of these goals, which are not necessarily mutually exclusive, and other purposes enunciated in various plans. Examples from actual programs are given in later chapters.

The Interest Doctrine

Teachers are often frustrated by the able student who is failing because he or she has no interest in school. It is a commonplace to observe that people learn more easily when they are interested. Some educators even feel that school programs should be oriented around the interests of the student. Parents, too, have experienced this situation, when John and Jane are "too tired" or "too busy" to do some chore around the house but suddenly find the energy and time to undertake a project outside with their friends. How can the curriculum maker capitalize upon students' natural tendency to put forth time and energy when they are interested? One way is to replace few year-long traditional courses with a variety of many, short, up-to-date minicourses that offer an opportunity to tap interests of both students and teachers.

The primary goal of minicourses is to involve students in an action-oriented program that is keyed to their interests. Through exposure to many different concepts, children acquire a broader base of knowledge. The minicourse program in the elementary schools of one Pennsylvania rural district started from a discussion among fourth and fifth grade teachers. Disappointed in the textbooks and feeling that the children were not really involved in their history lessons, these teachers wanted to put fun back into school. They felt that variety was needed for stimulation, and they found that a five-week minicourse program on several different subjects in both social studies and science added the needed variety.

A high school in a small town in southern California offered a minicourse program in the basic disciplines to encourage the teaching of subjects of particular interest to teachers and students and to urge students to delve into academic areas for the purpose of encouraging creative approaches to knowledge, interdisciplinary studies, and team-teaching methods. A suburban school system in Virginia established a minicourse program in their high school to give both students and teachers more independence. They wanted to give students the freedom to develop their individuality, skills, and new interests, and to discover the power of language. They wanted teachers to have time to share strengths and make decisions about the literature they were best qualified to teach, both by professional preparation and special interest.

Improvement of Instruction

The minicourse concept provides a way to open up the curriculum and to improve instruction. Although many schools grappling with the approach have included better teaching as an attainable goal with minicourses, encouraging teachers to follow their interests in developing courses will not necessarily evoke interest on the part of the students. A teacher may be a devotee of Chaucer, but the topic, in spite of the teacher's background and enthusiasm, may not draw sufficient enrollment. Nevertheless, the minicourse rationale at some schools is that students will develop interest in a two-to-six week course if an enthusiast teaches the class. Faculty members, as well as students in a school, could teach from special knowledge everything from fly fishing to the philosophy of Karl Marx.

When programs of the non-credit variety are offered, instructors are given the opportunity to teach courses in which they have a personal interest rather than just those that are part of their usual assigned areas. Furthermore, the non-credit offerings permit teachers to move into areas of interest that may not be related to their certified background. This is one way to make greater use of faculty talents. The staid mathematics teacher may be a scuba-diving expert, a gourmet cook, a creator of puzzles and designs, or a fledgling Fischer.

Most schools have some teacher turnover each year. When a teacher is transferred to another school or moves out of the district, who can replace his or her areas of strength? In a traditional program, seniority usually takes over; thus the new teacher is assigned to whatever position is open in the "pecking order" without necessarily utilizing his or her strengths in relation to school or student needs. A fluid offering of minicourses, however, might mean that a course formerly taught by the teacher who left could be transferred to another teacher who has a similar interest, or be dropped and replaced by a new course built on the strengths of the new teacher.

Because developing minicourses takes time, effort, and careful planning, schools rely heavily on in-service programs that themselves use the mini format. The microteaching technique promoted by Dwight Allen* and others from Stanford University provides the thrust for many of the minicourse programs designed for both pre-service and in-service operations. The purpose of each minicourse in this format is to provide directions, materials, and activities so that a teacher may learn a specific set of teaching skills—such as how to ask better questions.

The Far West Laboratory for Educational Research and Development developed a guide to go with a series of minicourse packages.† Some of the minicourses are:

— Divergent Thinking
— Individualizing Instruction in Mathematics

*Dwight Allen and K. Ryan, *Microteaching* (Palo Alto, Calif.: Addison-Wesley, 1969).

†These are available commercially through Macmillan Educational Corp., 866 Third Ave., New York, N.Y. 10022.

— Teaching Reading as Decoding
— Role Playing for Upper Elementary Grades.

Each minicourse consists of filmed or taped instructional materials, handbooks, evaluation forms, daily course schedules, and anything else required to conduct the course. A teacher devotes 55 to 75 minutes a day for seven to nine days to microteaching and reteaching in a small room with small groups of students, thus practicing the skills demonstrated on film. Each microteaching session is videotaped for later evaluation.

This minicourse package allows, then, for highly individualized learning, both in the choice of "course" and in the method of presentation. Active participation by the teacher is paramount since they are being "told" only about 10 percent of the time and are being "shown" only about 20 percent of the time. Thus 70 percent of the teacher's effort may be devoted to actual "doing," i.e., planning lessons, microteaching, and reteaching.

In a similar vein, the Florida Department of Education has developed individualized, performance-based teacher education programs. Called the "Model for Packaged Teacher Training Modules," these programs are aimed at helping school districts upgrade the qualifications of teachers who lack professional credentials or who, although certified, would like to improve certain skills. There are some 50 or so modules available for teacher aides as well as for regular teachers. They include:

— Recognizing How Children Develop
— Increasing Participation
— Feedback
— Fostering Creativity
— Developing Listening Skills

An interesting variation of in-service improvement using a minicourse approach was created by the social studies department at a suburban Philadelphia high school. The department set up 10 day-long sessions to enable social studies teachers to update themselves and to study various instructional phases such as lesson organization, teaching strategies, and program evaluation. A unique aspect of this endeavor was that the teachers participated during a regular school day while their classes were being taught by administrators and visiting teachers. The replacement teachers offered a specially designed series of minicourses tailored to the interests of the individual substitutes. The minicourses offered covered a wide range of subjects: Mid-East tensions, local politics, state elections, the national scene. The plan allowed program enrichment for the students by exposing them to the views and expertise of school and community people who would not otherwise have taught classes. It also met the perennial problem of time for in-service groups to get together and had an additional side benefit —the teachers built a greater rapport with each other. They freely shared their ideas about teaching, realizing their common concerns and offering each other help.

The free-form experience,* usually of just a few days, can be looked upon as an avenue to better teaching. Short, free-form experiments help teachers discover a new role—that of facilitator rather than information giver. Teachers can view themselves as colearners rather than as the sole purveyors of truth and knowledge. Moreover, these in-service minicourses offer teachers an opportunity for innovative teaching. Thus the role of the teacher becomes one of coordinating the learning environment and the experiences of the students.

A Minicourse for Substitute Teachers

Too often substitute teachers are faced with a classroom for which there are no prepared lesson plans, or the regular teacher's plans are not sufficiently clear for someone else to use. Sometimes the materials necessary to carry out the teacher's plans are missing. Working under an Education Professions Development Act project, the New Orleans public schools developed a corps of elementary grade substitute teachers prepared to deal with these problems. They did it by offering a minicourse, a one-month summer institute, for a group of substitute teachers. The participants in the program were assured of daily employment either as teachers, teacher aides, or office workers. The substitute teachers had to

---

*Ventures in education, as well as in business and industry, bring a satellite of special terms with them. Those surrounding the minicourse concept will be discussed in chapter two.

agree to accept assignments every day that they were able to work. The substitutes who completed the course became members of the Relief Teacher Corps. The title "relief teacher" distinguished them from other substitutes who had not had this special training.

All persons participating in the project developed a unit of study, dubbed micro-resource units, that they could adapt to whatever classroom they might be assigned to. During the summer's minicourse, the relief teachers acquainted themselves with related topics, themes, problems, and materials appropriate to their micro-units. These units were to supply significant instruction for one to several days, or even longer should the situation warrant it.

The goals of this minicourse were to develop a ready corps of substitute teachers and to increase the substitute's competence and pupil learning in the absence of the regular teacher. The relief teachers reported that after the training they perceived their roles in a new perspective. From this "mini practicum" and the coordinator's guidance, they gained more confidence and new skills for assuming the responsibilities of substitute teaching.

Developing Student Responsibility

The cooperative approach in curriculum development provides a chance for growth for all who participate—students, professional educators, and community members. The more one participates—whether it be in suggesting, developing, choosing, or evaluating—the more readily one will accept the new program. Genuine participation tends to generate a "psychological ownership" of the resulting product. To this end, many schools have included student involvement in decision-making as a major reason for creating minicourses. Even more schools have specifically endorsed the purpose of fostering independence and responsibility. They argue that the right to make choices and then to live with the consequences of those choices is an effective way for a young person to learn to take responsibility. The assumption is that presenting a variety of short-term electives provides students with practical experience in meeting a function of citizenship in our society—that of making thoughtful decisions about their personal goals when faced with several alternatives.

A traditional curriculum that moves to a curriculum with options may well be the beginning of a student's learning to assume responsibility for his or her own education. While some raise the question "Is the student ready?" experience shows that a carefully planned program, one that incorporates the options of counsel and assistance, can be undertaken by learners at any age. As will be noted later, some high schools "trust" the juniors and seniors, but not the sophomores. Elementary schools "trust" fifth and sixth graders, but not the younger students. As expressed by a junior high school in Ohio, the idea is that every individual should be stimulated to become self-directing:

> Students learn best when they are personally involved in the learning process; when they have a choice in the establishment of goals and objectives; when they can be involved in the solving of immediate problems which have meaning in their own lives. Students should be offered opportunities for making decisions and experience the consequences of their decision making. The educational program should allow students options and alternative choices among goals, methods, and materials and these selections should be respected by adults with whom they work.*

The whole concept of phasing (or levels) provides the student with a chance for self-assessment: "What decisions should I make in terms of the opportunities available?" The student may make a mistake and be stuck with a course for a few weeks, but that is better than being in the wrong course for a whole year.

Learning by Variation

If we accept the belief that learning is a result of a variety of contacts, then it follows that during the school year the student should be exposed to a variety of teachers with differing philosophies, backgrounds, and strategies of instruction. As schools seek to individualize instruction, they find merit in matching teaching styles to student learning styles. In the past, high school students with five subjects spent five days a week for some 40 weeks with the same five teachers and the same classmates. An elective-quarter

*From the curriculum philosophy of Roehm Junior High School, Berea, Ohio.

system offers the potential of four different teachers and changing groups of classmates for each subject in the same time span. To some degree, the personality clashes that might otherwise develop between student and teacher or among students could be avoided.

The quarter system exposes a student to new individuals as well as to new teachers and experiences. Any school operates as a society, and even a moderate sized school of 1,000 to 1,200 can be impersonal. Quarters allow the students to meet four times as many of their fellows in the course of a year. This is particularly important in a school of 2,000 or more students.

Increasing the Scope and Depth of the Curriculum

A major problem confronting schools is how to keep up with the explosion of knowledge. This factor, tied to accelerating social change, creates curriculum problems for all schools, especially for those with a limited staff. Here, particularly, minicourses show maximum potential. Dividing the school year into quarters means that the curriculum can be expanded fourfold. In language arts and the social sciences a number of short-term courses can be offered each quarter, some perhaps repeated during the year and others replaced the next quarter by a different course.

Social studies, too often an unpopular subject, can be made more interesting by allowing students to choose from a variety of subdivisions in the field and by offering courses that deal with the present and future as well as the past. (Examples of the tremendous variety for these and other subjects are presented in chapters four and five.) Not all subjects, notably mathematics and foreign languages, can easily be broken into short-term electives, but a little imagination can present a lot of variety, even here.

The opening up of the curriculum by means of the minicourse has actually meant a modification of subject matter boundaries. Topics and themes built upon student and/or teacher interests are often interdisciplinary in nature. School systems studying the year-round school concept have found that the resulting wide range of courses increases the opportunity for teachers to cooperate with their counterparts in other departments. The result is an increase in the depth as well as in the scope of the curriculum. Certainly the minicourse can be a dimension stretcher.

In another way, a student's personal scope may be increased. With short-term options students can readily take courses beyond the minimum requirements. Under the traditional organization, most students would find it difficult to take two year-long English courses at the same time, even if they were available. Under the quarter plan the student can take four courses a year and might be able to add a fifth course for one quarter. Then, during a later quarter, the student could select an extra minicourse from another subject field.

The minicourse allows small schools to expand their curriculum. A Missouri school with 50 students and five full-time faculty members is able to use some occasional teachers from the community by dividing their academic year into five seven-week terms. At the beginning of each term, students consult their advisor and select the courses they wish to take during the ensuing term. Short-term courses allow students to choose from a rich variety of offerings and enable the school to utilize the skills of professional volunteers from the community who usually are not available on a year or even a semester basis.

Elementary schools and especially junior high schools speak of their desire to help the students "find themselves." One way to do this is by offering "exploratory" minicourses on a non-graded basis, particularly appropriate for pre-vocational or foreign language courses. These learning experiences expose students to ideas and topics not usually found in the school curriculum. Hobbies and leisure-time activities can also be covered effectively and new interests stimulated among students. In junior high schools some administrators see the minicourse as a way to add variety to their programs and thus enhance the "exploratory" function of the junior high.

Student interest and teacher strength indicate a preference for depth as well as for variety. Short courses, by their nature, have to be limited; a common practice is to build each course around a single topic or theme rather than to try to be comprehensive. Thus an individual minicourse, though limited in scope, may be extensive in depth. The intent is to investigate, to learn about, and to understand a limited area. This might suggest an intensive look at the "literature of the occult" or "rock poetry."

"Ecology" and "people and the city" are other topics of increasing interest and concern.

As in most ventures, an advantage can become a disadvantage. A program loaded with in-depth minis can become a highly seasoned smorgasbord which, if sampled unwisely, can lead to intellectual indigestion. Balance between scope and depth, then, is a caution for the curriculum-maker as well as for the curriculum-consumer. The mini approach offers tremendous opportunities in scope (quantity) and depth (quality) to all schools regardless of size. The courses for credit may greatly increase in number and in focus. "Free-form" opportunities provide a chance to enrich the regular program as well to explore student interests for possible future study. The key words are: variety, enrichment, depth, exploration, and expansion.

Community Ties

"Horizontal articulation," the interaction between the school and its community, is a fundamental principle of curriculum improvement. Mini programs have great potential as articulation agencies and many schools have built this concept into the perceived purposes of their plans for elective offerings. This is not to say that a traditional program cannot be community-related, but that short-term elective courses and free-form experiments have basic variation and flexibility that enchance this desired relationship.

The conventional school, both in its conception and physical structure, is in a sense withdrawn from the community. Rather than plunge the learner directly into the maelstrom of life, it is argued, the school selects from life and, in its sheltered environment, presents its selection to the student. This practice, however, makes "in-school learning" unnecessarily abstract and theoretical. Learners need the concrete to give meaning to the verbal and abstract courses of the school. Bringing the community into the school and the school into the community facilitate one understanding the other. Though communities vary in their resources, no community is devoid of unique people, places, and institutions. Students should have an opportunity to learn what is noteworthy about or characteristic of their own community. Mini offerings recognize that learning occurs in many places; trips to local industries, organizations, and historic sites take advantage of these aspects of the community outside the school building.

A free-form program gives a school a chance to experiment with different programs and different instructional ideas. Off-campus learning centers, organized with the assistance of local institutions and businesses, can do this well. Adults outside the school can add a new dimension to students' learning experiences. Other adults can be invited to take courses in the school. Both are a good way to enhance rapport between the school and townspeople, parents and students. Such programs result in an increased relevance of the school's efforts to the community, enhance the the possibility that students can develop life-long interests, and develop confidence in the school by its patrons.

Parent information meetings are another important aspect of a community-outreach curriculum. They can be used to let parents know about opportunities to volunteer their services in a school's library and resource centers and to serve as instructors of minicourses. A junior high school in Connecticut used such a gathering to enlist parents as teachers of minicourses. Parents volunteered to give minicourses, to be offered during a class period once a day for one week only, which included the following:

— A nursing home administrator on "How We Can Help the Elderly"
— A local T.B. association official on "Why Smoke?"
— An airline employee on "Opportunities in the Air"
— A florist on "Floral Designing"
— A local university professor on "Black History and Culture"

Good community ties are especially important if a year-round program is being considered. Parents must understand how this might affect their family plans, especially vacations. Local industries and businesses will be affected by having employable youth available at different times of the year. The curriculum itself must be restructured to place an increasing amount of responsibility on the learner as it uses the community as an expanded classroom. It is vital to continue and expand active involvement of all segments of the community in the affairs of the school district as it moves to a year-round pattern.

Many Motives

It may seem contradictory to use the terms "many" and "mini" together. Yet a study of the documents from schools offering or planning these curriculum alternatives indicate many purposes, both major and minor, in addition to those already covered. A list of these suggest possible directions for others wanting to revitalize their educational programs. Flexibility is a feature desired in any program and is specifically mentioned in most minicourse proposals. Minis can be of varying lengths; they can be offered, withheld, or dropped as the situation warrants. They may or may not be offered for credit or grades. They can be in one academic field, interdisciplinary, or simply beyond the ordinary offerings. In addition to this flexibility there are other goals desired by schools instituting minicourses. Some are offshoots of goals already discussed. These other common goals include the following:

— Relieve boredom
— Increase enrollment (particularly in foreign languages)
— Reflect a spirit of change
— Enhance the self-concept of students, teachers, and other participants
— Ease assimilation of transfer students
— Provide a transition to a new type of curriculum
— Reduce the number of dropouts
— Eliminate repetition in courses
— Provide a better way to make up failed courses
— Improve student-teacher rapport
— Provide a vehicle for curriculum review
— Enhance opportunities for experimentation
— Eliminate tracking and/or provide non-graded programs
— Provide opportunities for individual acceleration
— Reduce discipline problems.

Some Underlying Assumptions
for the Minicourse

Good programs require thoughtful purposes. The goals and programs described in this chapter suggest certain underlying assumptions that the curriculum planner should be aware of before embarking on the minicourse venture. Some of these assumptions are given below.

— The program should, as Dewey put it, be based on "learning by experience, motivated by a sense of the student's needs."

— Learning is a highly individual process.

— Teachers teach better when they have courses based on their interests.

— Depth is preferable to breadth.

— There should be a balance, according to Alfred North Whitehead's ideal, between "the spirit of change and the spirit of conservation. There can be nothing real without both. Mere conservation without change cannot conserve; mere change without conservation is a passage from nothing to nothing."

— Exposure to the real world is essential to meaningful learning.

— Within certain grade ranges, courses should be open to all.

— Each individual should be stimulated to become self-directing.

— Learning does not take place in a systematic and orderly manner. Students do not learn most efficiently when knowledge is compartmentalized and segmented; they learn best when information is interrelated, and when given opportunities to apply what has been learned to the solving of problems.

— Students learn from each other as well as from teachers.

— Not all students need to learn the same things.

— Any *one* instructional style will induce boredom in most students.

— A human being is, among other things, a curious animal and, given a sufficient degree of freedom, will attempt to satisfy that curiosity at a pace that avoids both frustration and boredom.

— Students should have input into curriculum planning.

— A person's attitudes affect the way he or she perceives.

— The chance to choose increases motivation.

— Students need practice in making important decisions.

— Although the concept of prerequisite requirements has validity in some instances, the segmented pattern in some disciplines is not defensible.

— There are certain subjects that do not need to be as lengthy as a semester or a school year.

— Students and teachers benefit from a "change of pace."

— Minicourses are well suited for facilitating educational innovations and for the piloting of new programs.

In summary, if we are not to become obsolete ourselves we must keep on learning, unlearning, and relearning. Teachers should want their students to become learners, not knowers, and a well-planned and thoughtful minicourse program can aid this effort.

References

Allen, Dwight, and Ryan, K. *Microteaching*. Palo Alto: Addison-Wesley, 1969.

Bunker, R. "Beyond Inservice: Toward Staff Renewal," *Journal of Teacher Education* 28:31-34 (March-April 1977).

DeSistri, Sam. "MUE: Mini-Unit Experience," *NASSP Bulletin* 55:75-78 (March 1971).

Gove, James R. *Final Report on Project No. 1-E-114*, "A Feasibility Study of the 45-15 Plan for Year-Round Operation of a Public High School Served by an Elementary District (Valley View #96, Will County, State of Illinois) Already on the

45-15 Plan." Romeoville, Illinois: Valley View School District #96, 1972.

Guenther, John, and Ridgway, Robert. "Minicourses: Promising Alternative in the Social Studies," *Clearing House* 47:486-89 (April 1973).

_____"Minicourses in Junior High Schools," *School and Community* 61:10-11 (April 1975).

Gyves, J.J., and Clark, D.C. "The Interest-Centered Curriculum: Is Interest Enough?" *Clearing House* 49:33-36 (September 1975).

Heitzmann, William Ray. *Minicourses.* Washington, D.C.: National Education Association, 1977.

Hutchins, C.L., et al. *Minicourses Work.* Berkeley: Far West Laboratory for Educational Research and Development, n.d.

Jennings, Wayne. *Design Rationale and Implementation of the St. Paul Open School.* St. Paul: Minnesota Public Schools, 1971.

Oliver, Albert I. *Curriculum Improvement,* 2nd Ed. New York: Harper and Row Company, 1977, Chapter II.

Parsons, R.C. "Ungraded English," *Clearing House* 41:533-35 (May 1967).

Pirsig, Nancy. "Bumpy Open Road to the Open School," *American Education* 8:17-23 (October 1972).

Rugg, Harold, and Shumaker, Ann. *The Child-Centered School.* New York: Arno Press, 1969.

Russell, I.L. "Development of Attitudes, Interests and Values," *Educational Psychology,* Edited by C.E. Skinner. Englewood Cliffs: Prentice-Hall, 1961.

Chapter 2

WHAT IS A MINICOURSE?

A school that is not experimenting is educationally dead. A school that experiments without careful planning that involves all faculty (and students) associated with the project is wasteful of time and effort. Experimentation that does not involve day-to-day and week-to week assessment and change is constipated. Experimentation that does not involve evaluation of the program's success is mute.

—*Maurice Gibbons*
Simon Fraser University

The minicourse has emerged in a variety of forms, each with a particular purpose in mind. Though its variations suggest a number of meanings for minicourse, the concept has two basic elements: the courses are short-term and elective. Short-term has come to mean almost any time span shorter than the basic school year. Time spans for minicourses vary from one to three days, from three weeks to a month, these latter often during an intersession. For credit courses, the quarter length is most common. Even some semester courses take the mini approach. Another time slot where minis fit in is a student's "free-time" such as study hall periods when a series of minicourses can be offered over a particular block of time. Elective means that the student has options. A student may select a course from a certain group of courses in a particular subject area. Though students may be restricted to courses at their grade level, they most typically can choose any alternative courses offered school wide.

Minicourses emphasize an attempt at curriculum improvement, a way to better teaching-learning situations. Paramount is the elective nature of the offerings, which tend to be student-focused in nature. There is much student involvement in planning and execution and, since teachers also suggest courses based on their interests, there is an opportunity to build upon faculty strengths. This is often enhanced by community involvement of varying degrees. "Curriculum" is conceived of in a broad sense; although the most effective and lasting minicourses are academic, many minicourse activities are non-academic and some are non-credit. In short, the best minicourses are based upon sound curriculum foundations.

Minicourse Terminology

In education today, the term "mini" has many meanings. Though it has a Latin root meaning small, emerging practices in schools around the country indicate that the term applied to courses has maximum potential. In recent years the minicourse has become a major alternative to traditional organization of the curriculum and to standard course offerings. Indeed, the minicourse concept has emerged as an excellent way to open up the curriculum and to bring about changes in course content. Minicourses can increase learner participation, introduce new teaching-learning strategies, and facilitate the "re-education" of teachers themselves.

The term mini has also been used for educational ventures other than courses. The mini-school has been proposed as an alternative form of organization for urban elementary schools, and the mini-grant has come to be applied to small grants, particularly those funded by Title I of the Elementary and Secondary Education Act. The mini-school, as a protest against the dehumanizing aspects of large school units, parallels the minicourse as a protest against the formality of year-long courses. The mini-grant, as funding for a limited, specific project in a school system, parallels the use of the term mini for a limited, specific course in a variety of subject areas.

A number of threads in the minicourse movement have been around for a long time, but these threads were not really woven

into a productive curriculum pattern until the social upheaval of
the 1960s persuaded schools, along with many other institutions,
to take hard looks at themselves. One of these threads is the elective courses in such subjects as journalism, debate, music, and
typing which have long been offered by secondary schools, although these courses have often been considered "second class,"
carrying only partial credit. Another thread was the concern for
the individual that is part of the philosophies of most schools. Still
another thread was the importance of the interest factor
long noted by psychologists. The mini-movement has moved many
"second-class" courses into "first-class" position and offered full
credit for some. It has also moved concern for the individual from
verbiage to action. The mini-movement has enhanced the interest
factor for students *and* teachers by giving both a chance to make
choices, in courses taken and in courses taught, related to their
own interest.

The development of alternative programs was hastened when
relevance became a curriculum watchword and when the principle
of tying education to the concerns of students became important
in curriculum planning. During this period curriculum developers
were also forced to became more responsive to critics like John
Holt, Ivan Illich, William Glasser, Charles Silberman and others
who argued that educational programs and practices were dehumanizing. Minicourses, by allowing students to make their own
choices, by involving students and teachers in planning and in
evaluating, were seen as steps to rehumanizing the classroom.

The results of a decade and more of intense activity was that
the fabric of American education was rewoven to reflect the desire
of students to have choices available, and to be able to make their
own decisions about these options. The creation of the Educational Alternatives Projects by the Indiana School of Education
crystallized this movement. The project was a motivating force
in establishing a National Consortium on Educational Alternatives.*

The minicourse concept has given rise to a series of acronyms
used by various school systems to describe innovative practices:
SCIP for Short Course Insertion Program, PEP for Personalized

*For a thorough discussion of this movement, see Allan A. Glatthorn, Ed.,
Alternatives in Education: Schools and Progress (New York: Dodd, Mead,
1975).

Educational Participation, APEX for Appropriate Placement for Excellence in English, and STEN for Student-Teacher Educational Needs. All these are attempts to depart from the conventional pattern of year-long courses. All reflect a desire to introduce new courses, new topics, and new experiences closely related to student interests in a rapidly changing economy.

Two other terms that give further dimension to the minicourse concept and suggest some alternatives to consider in instituting a minicourse program are "free-form" and "phase-electives." Often called "effie," the acronym EFFE refers to Experiment in Free Form Education. This "free-form" approach intends to offer students, faculty, and community members an opportunity to plan together and to participate in short explorations of areas that may be adjunct to or actually outside the conventional program of studies. These free-form courses are usually short, often intensive, investigations of a particular aspect of a subject area or a brief overview of subject-matter outside the traditional curriculum. They are found in both elementary and high schools. Usually no credits or marks are involved.

The term "phase electives," often called "levels," refers to the relative difficulty of a course, and hence the amount of effort and ability needed to complete that course successfully. This movement, found particularly in secondary school English, has replaced tracking or grouping in many school systems. In phasing, the school personnel determine the difficulty level of a course rather than concentrate on the presumed ability of the students. A common practice is to indicate "phases" on a scale from one to five, with Phase 1 for the student with limited skills and Phase 5, which often includes materials and approaches that require high levels of proficiency, for advanced students. The student, with the aid of a counsellor, chooses a course commensurate with his or her knowledge and skill in a particular field. These courses are usually found only in high schools.

In most secondary schools, English departments have taken the lead in instituting short-term elective courses, often after hearing the idea discussed at annual conventions of the National Council of Teachers of English. Since the late 1960s, NCTE conventions have had several programs dealing with elective English courses and other course alternatives have been written about in *English Journal.* In many schools where English electives have been established, the social studies department explores the idea a year or two later. The physical education, home economics, art, and science departments soon follow.

One cannot talk about ungraded programs without recalling the work done by H. Frank Brown while he was principal of Melbourne High School in Florida. Although Brown's 1963 suggestion that the school organization of the future would be ungraded, elementary school through college, may not have been a realistic projection, notions that he pioneered then have become common practices in many schools. Brown also introduced the term "phase." Though used in many different ways today, it is interesting to look at the concept as presented by Brown in the early 1960s.

> The plan for continuous learning at Melbourne accommodates youngsters by placing them in temporary learning situations from which they can move at any time. These ad hoc learning arrangements are called "phases." A phase is a state of development with a varying time element. One student may remain in a lower phase indefinitely; another may progress rapidly into higher phases. The prime vehicle in a program of educational diversity is mobility. The student must find the paths to deeper learning always open.
>
> When students enter Melbourne high school, they are sorted on the basis of nationally standardized achievement tests. They are then clustered into the phase spectrum in line with their varying aptitudes and abilities.
>
> The object of shifting from age grouping to achievement grouping is to devise an educational program suited to the individual needs and capacities of each student. No youngster at Melbourne is programmed in a common design; each is scheduled as an individual. Students at Melbourne are academically rearranged out of the grade lockstep and into five cycles of learning, or phases. These phases are learning dimensions designed to group students in relation to their knowledge or skills: low, minimal, medium, high, superior.*

*H. Frank Brown, *The Nongraded High School* (Englewood Cliffs, N.J.: Prentice-Hall, 1963), p. 49-50.

From Brown's pioneering efforts in the early 1960s, through the upheavals of the rest of the decade and beyond, the minicourse evolved, with its satellites of terms and concepts, and manners or methods of organization. The general format the minicourse has taken, time spans and specific advantages of each, will be discussed in the rest of this chapter. Chapter three offers details on how one goes about developing a minicourse program.

The Lengths of a Minicourse

As one contacts schools around the country concerning their minicourse offerings, one finds many variations. Basically, the uses of the term "mini" in schools show the derivative meaning of "small" or "less" and encompass a range from a short unit (maybe a part of a traditional course, maybe a part of an innovative offering) to a full semester. Following are variations with illustrations from actual school practices. Characteristic of most plans is the principle that the student has choices.

One Day

A number of schools use a special one-day program as an opening wedge to curriculum variation. Some administrators also see this as an opportunity to identify instructional approaches that might later be included in the regular program. Usually, the one-day mini program means that the regular school program is suspended so that students may have the opportunity to attend seminars on a variety of subjects conducted by a variety of discussion leaders. There may be several seminar periods of about an hour-and-a-half duration. School on that day is "different": different teachers, ranging from the school superintendent to volunteer community members, and different ideas to argue and think about. Intriguing program titles in schools that have tried this approach include:

How to Succeed in School Without Cheating
Are You a Revolutionary or Merely Revolting?

Don't Be Stuck Up Anymore: Drug Therapy
It's a Real Steal: Shoplifting
Coffee, Tea, or Milk? Airline Stewardess
Barbed Wire Society—Ex-Prisoners Help Themselves
Life Among the Rural Mennonites
Raising Praying Mantis for Fun and Profit
Backpacking

An interesting modification of the one-day-in-a-year program was tried out in a Nevada high school. For 15 weeks during the spring semester, one period a week was set aside for mini classes. The program included such diverse courses as: Happiness in Singing, Basic Welding, Think Tank, and Bumming across Europe. An Alaska high school ventured two consecutive days of enrichment with courses ranging from electronics to dog mushing, from swimming to Arctic survival.

These limited minis are usually offered on a no-credit, no-grade basis. Their purpose is to offer a free-wheeling learning experience without the usual restraints of course requirements and without the threat of grades. Fundamentally, the one-day mini provides an opportunity for students to participate in discussions on topics they have a personal interest in. To that extent, the plan is a mini-step toward personalization of the curriculum.

One Week

The one-week program is similar to the one-day offering both in organization and purpose: regular classes are suspended in order to vary the course offerings. Mini-week variations, however, provide a school with more opportunities for curriculum innovations. One spring an Indianapolis high school offered a "soul week" when all regular classes were suspended to allow students to explore many offerings. Another high school offered 350 special courses and work experiences in an "effie" week. As is characteristic in most of the free-form programs, student input into the courses was high and both students and community members became teachers along with the regular faculty.

If a decision is to be made to devote one week to minis from an entire school year, when should it be? Basically the decision rests upon the underlying purpose. If the main purpose is to present a "change of pace," mid-year is a good time. If it is a recognition of student slump, the restlessness associated with spring fever, a school might follow the approach taken by a California high school. They initiated a program called the Merry Month of May Mini Unit, a series of courses held on consecutive afternoons.

Another approach is to devote a mini-week to one particular theme or project. Two one-week projects were scheduled during the course of the year at a high school in Alaska. One week was devoted to an all-school, multi-age group environmental project. All formal classes were cancelled and replaced with one- and two-hour seminars on various aspects of environmental concerns. These classes were taught by teachers, local citizens, and the U.S. Forest Service. During the week, in addition to attending the seminars, students painted houses, tore down old buildings, cleaned up city streets and public and private yards and beaches.

A private girls school in Ohio set aside a mini-week for travel. The purpose of the trips—to such places as Boston, New Orleans, and London, and a hosteling journey through Pennsylvania—was education outside the class, education by insertion into the community, and education by experience rather than by reading.

In a junior high school outside Boston, teachers and students tried a week-long minicourse at the end of the school year to provided a year-end spree for fun and learning. Half of a student's program had to be in an academic area and there was a limit of two sport courses per pupil. The diversified program included such selections as languages, gymnastics, rocketry, marine biology, sailing, yoga, and cake decorating. Junior high school youngsters have a lot of energy and, at the end of a school year especially, this energy seeks channels other than the daily routine. A mini-week, whether placed at mid-year or at year's end, provides an opportunity to experiment with different "courses" and to see how student energy and activity can be utilized in program development. Often this one-week venture will provide the stimulus to try longer mini programs.

Three Weeks

The block of time of three, or perhaps four, weeks presents some interesting mini options. How might this time be used? Some schools use a three-week intensive interval in conjunction with their academic program, thus offering electives for which a student might receive credit.

The "basics plus" concept at an Alabama high school calls for scheduling all English classes by grade level for a designated number of weeks. Various selections of literature are read and discussed in regular classes. At the end of the allotted time, students are rescheduled into one of three skill areas—reading, grammar, or composition—or into an elective. Placement in the skills classes is based on scores made on diagnostic tests given in the year. After the students have worked up to a desired level of proficiency in each of the skill areas, they may substitute an elective minicourse for a skills class. Examples of minicourses offered include mass media, mythology, drama or poetry, an in-depth study of a particular author, and contemporary novels. Selected students may work on an independent project at this time and are not assigned to a class. At the end of approximately three weeks, students return to their regular English classes and the cycle begins again.

The social studies department in a Pennsylvania high school used a three-week slot from the end of October to mid-November for a variation they called "Section Switch by Method." During this time freshmen and sophomores could select a course according to teaching style. The students were allowed to choose which teacher they wanted to work with, a decision based on the teacher's style—either traditional or adventurous. At the end of this three-week period, the students returned to their usual teachers and regular classrooms.

The English department in an Indiana high school used another approach to the three-week block. Students in grades 10, 11, and 12 were offered three-week minicourses during the first three weeks of school and again during the last three weeks. The two minicourse periods were decided on because in the fall students are more alert and so are the teachers, so everyone was ready for some rewarding challenges. In the spring, during the last three weeks of school, the students are often bored and so are the teachers; the department offered a mini program to end the year on a high note.

The Interim

A special form of the three- or four-week mini is the interim or intersession—a month set aside for special programs between the fall and spring semesters. This approach is now used in many colleges and a few secondary schools have experimented with the interim idea as well. The minicourse program of a private high school in San Francisco occupies the month of January. Certain courses that are a part of the normal curriculum are held in the morning; the rest of the day is divided into hour-and-a-half mods during which students may choose between a variety of mini-courses, which meet daily (ceramics), two days a week (accelerated reading, advanced music), or three days a week (French cooking, psychology, new directions in education). Some seniors spend the whole month off campus in other parts of the United States or in Europe. Others become involved with individual projects in the San Francisco area or spend part of their week in independent study.

January can be a "lame duck" period and a mini approach can eliminate the lack of focus often associated with the month. The interim period at a private, innovative girls' school in South Dakota began as a "future week" during which normal classes were suspended. The students, faculty, and staff, acting as a community, participated in an all-school, mosaic probing of the future called "Future Week: Make Space in Your Brains for Tomorrow." As a result of this experience, the interim was expanded into a three-week program, illustrating another potential of the mini-approach: start small and expand as you learn how to deal with the innovations.

Most schools see the interim as an integral part of the school year, and all students are expected to participate. Some schools give credit and grades (pass/fail is most common in these situations); others see the period as one of enrichment free from the pressure of marks. Notations on the student's record will be of value later on.

The essence of the interim organization is that it provides educational opportunities not usually available during conventional semesters. The student selects one topic, project, or "course" to investigate in depth during the three-to-four-week period. Usually students welcome this as a chance to explore some area that does not fit in with their regular program. Some use the opportunity to do remedial work.

Free Time

Various studies* have confirmed what many teachers already know—study halls for those not in class are relatively unprofitable for students. Consequently, more and more schools are moving to an "open campus" concept. Under this system, when students do not have a class, they are free to come and go. Other schools have modified the plan, giving students several options during "unassigned time," with the qualification that they may not leave the campus. Increasingly these options include a chance to enroll in some mini-course available during one's "free time."

In these cases it is common for the offerings to be student-developed and, in many cases, student-taught. Usually the courses provide enrichment through experiences excluded from the regular courses: chess, auto safety, poodle grooming, gardening, and personal problems. These mini-courses are often a good way to capture the attention of students who have not learned to use study hall time productively.

A junior high school in Wisconsin took an unusually innovative approach by initiating five-day minicourses for students during their study hall assignments. Participating teachers were required to give up one preparation period a week each semester, an act taken only after a poll had indicated a high level of staff interest. The teachers were asked to submit topical outlines for the minicourses they wanted to offer. For students, the arrangement was

*Those by Blumenfeld and Remmer, Draayer and Teagner, and Streitmatter are particularly interesting and are listed in the References section at the end of this chapter.

simple—they enrolled in a minicourse rather than attending study hall, and five days later either signed up for another minicourse or returned to study hall. Enrollment in these courses was limited to 10 students. No tests or grades were given, but certificates of satisfactory completion were issued. To encourage community involvement, parents were asked to approve their child's choice of minicourses and to list courses they might like to teach. The courses scheduled included map projects, gardening, decoupage, slide rule, needlecraft, auto and small boat safety, Wisconsin Indians, tropical fish, poodle grooming, macrame, home electrical repair, and current issues. These courses were found to be particularly beneficial for students who didn't particularly enjoy school —the minicourse made their day!

Many schools now schedule minicourses during lunch periods, as well as during free time. A school with a divided lunch period can schedule a series of short courses of two-week duration for one half of the lunch period. Students are seldom required to take such mini-courses, but schools offering them find that about half of the students do.

Another non-classroom time often used for minicourses is the homeroom period. An Indiana high school uses its daily 52-minute homeroom for two purposes: Mondays, Wednesdays, and Fridays are for minicourses, Tuesdays and Thursdays for clubs. The minicourse program is non-credit; instructors are the faculty or student volunteers who excel in a particular skill. The school found that their students preferred activities that used their hands to rap-type sessions. One semester, student experts offered leathercraft, bicycling, and spelunking; and faculty members offered religions of the world, American contributions to the theatre, and ethics.

Quarter Courses

The majority of the organizational arrangements discussed so far have been of the non-credit, exploratory, enrichment variety. The nine-week quarter has become a popular way to reorganize year-long academic courses into shorter alternatives. These quarters are often tied to the length of the marking period.

Since many California secondary schools have had a semester pattern for many years, the quarter has become their short term. Administrators there see a switch to the quarter plan as one way to broaden the curriculum—to make more courses available to more students without increasing the number of teachers. A high school in the state of Washington, which has a school year divided into a 15-week first semester, a six-week "mini-quarter," and a 15-week second semester, offers what they call a "community-based instruction program." During the mini-quarter all 1,600 students must schedule themselves for 20 hours per week of special course offerings. Students select their preferred mini-quarter courses and community-based activities from a long and varied list of offerings, divided into on-campus classes, off-campus classes, and vocational exploratory activities. About half of the student body selects occupational-exploratory activities and job-intern experiences outside the school building. Course opportunities, both on and off campus, range from abacus to young lawyers.

Semester Courses

Although some might feel that semester offerings are not really minicourses, semester plans are included here for three reasons. First, since most elementary and secondary schools use year-long courses, the semester plan does represent a 50 percent cut in course length. Second, if the semester-length course is elective in nature, the semester course meets another condition of minicourses: that the student has choices. Third, if the step—albeit a cautious one—is undertaken as an opening wedge to curriculum revision, then it represents a major goal of the mini movement, which is trying out curriculum alternatives. Perhaps the plan for semester electives is a "maxi-mini," carrying with it some of the desired potential of the mini movement. A review of practices in various schools will show how and why.

It might be well be begin by looking at one format that shows a transition from semester to quarter, and ask the question: Is there any reason, other than administrative convenience, why all courses need to be the same length? A compromise between required courses and electives was made in a Pennsylvania high school where the school year was divided into semester and quarter courses for juniors and seniors in English and in social studies. During the first half of the year students take required semester courses; during the second half of the year students have two elective quarters. For example, during the fall English students take the key elements of the standard program—grammer, literature survey, composition, and vocabulary. During the two quarters, they can elect a course from a variety of offerings, from intensive studies of literature to remedial composition.

The semester can also serve as a pilot period for a new idea. A suburban Chicago high school launched an experimental program with a trial period of one summer session and the fall semester, with its continuation into the spring semester dependent upon the results of the fall semester. One purpose of the program was to provide a time of experimentation for each student to find out how he or she learned best. To this end a procedure was established whereby students wrote "semester contracts." Each contract stated the subject chosen, the approach the student would take in his or her study, the resources to be used, and the system by which the student would be evaluated. The areas of study ranged from the traditional, such as plane geometry and world history, to the non-traditional, such as health foods and the comics. When a number of students were unable to plan their courses for an entire semester in advance, the program was modified and a system of six-week classes was substituted. These classes were then combined in different ways to complete a credit.

Schools that offer semester electives subscribe to the belief that full semester courses allow for greater breadth and depth of subject matter. Also, they feel that the semester provides more opportunity for better acquaintance between student and teacher, a point that is particularly valid in large schools and a supposition that will be further examined in chapter three.

Some Trends

The NEA *Research Bulletin* for May 1972 published a report of a nation-wide sampling of public schools that asked some questions about their approaches to free-form education. The survey found that, of those replying, about one school system in four offered minicourses. The following is a tabulation of replies to the question: Do schools in your system offer "free-form" or "minicourses" that are outside the regular curriculum and not for credit in which pupils pursue topics of their own interest?

Percent of School Districts Offering Minicourses

Kind of School	All Systems	Systems by Size of Enrollment		
		25,000 or more	3,000 to 25,000	Under 3,000
High School	18	34	26	15
Junior High School	7	16	13	15
Middle School	4	5	6	3
Elementary School	4	11	6	3
No Schools in System	78	59	67	81

Since that time several individual states have made studies of the trends in course offering in their public schools. The state education agency in New Jersey has reported that the number of new courses it has been asked to approve shows a clear trend toward minicourses—most frequently in English, but also in social studies and art.

John Guenther, of the University of Kansas, has conducted a series of studies, the latest of which was presented at the Association for Supervision and Curriculum Development meeting in Houston in March 1977, on minicourse offerings in four midwestern states—Iowa, Kansas, Missouri, and Nebraska. He found that the potential for flexibility and the possibilities for individualization within the minicourse format was meriting serious consideration by educators, teachers, and administrators.

In 1974 the Indiana Department of Public Instruction conducted a study of language arts offerings in the state's secondary schools. The goal was to determine the status of elective programs and elective courses. As in the Guenther survey, they found a steady movement to implement elective programs in the secondary schools. No one reported abandoning the minicourse approach once it had been tried.

The reports from these three sources coincide with the findings of the author—that more and more schools are moving to short-term electives, and that relatively few are abandoning them. From their 1972 study of elective English programs in the high schools of Ohio, Nichols and Wootton* predicted that by the end of the decade 70 percent of Ohio high schools would be offering electives of some kind.

Whether or not the minicourse remains a popular and practical curriculum innovation, the options it offers and the new notions it introduces will continue to have an impact on schools. In this chapter various minicourse formats found in schools across the United States have been identified to show what administrative arrangements are possible in providing curriculum alternatives, and in offering a change of pace. The interest in creating minicourses remains, although the meaning of the term keeps changing to meet new needs. What it means in a particular school system depends upon the curriculum maker's point of view. It depends upon his or her daring, imagination, and ability to cooperate with teachers. Students at one high school caught the spirit in their mini-week, calling it the "voice of change." Their program was prefaced by a song popular at the time in which change was defined as "not the same." The minicourse concept is sufficiently flexible to allow this to be as good a definition as any other.

---

*James R. Nichols and Verne B. Wootton, "The Ohio Survey of High School English Programs," *Ohio English Bulletin* 13:2-17 (March 1972).

References

Bain, Philip. "For a Real Change of Pace, Try It Once a Week," *Clearing House* 50:65 (October 1976).

Blumenfeld, Warren S., and Remmer, H.H. "Attitudes Toward Study Hall as Related to Grades," *Journal of Educational Research* 59:406-08 (1966).

Carlsen, G. Robert. "Some Random Observations—About the English Curriculum," *English Journal* 61:1004-07 (October 1972).

Draayer, Donald R., and Teagner, Patricia Ann. "Student Lounge or Study Hall—How Are Grades Affected?" *Clearing House* 44:141-44 (November 1969).

"Flirting with Free Forming?" *Nation's Schools* 90:25-28 (July 1972).

Graves, Richard L. "English Elective Curricula and How They Grew," *Educational Forum* 38:195-201 (January 1974).

Maimon, Morton. "The Mini School: Implications for Urban Elementary Education." Doctoral dissertation, University of Pennsylvania, 1972.

Mini School News, New York Urban Coalition, Inc., 55 Fifth Avenue, New York, N.Y. 10003.

Parkinson, Daniel S. "The Minicourse Approach in Ohio," *Phi Delta Kappan* 57:551-52 (April 1976).

Soyerand, Jim, and Giese, Sister Jeanne. "Future Week: Make Space in Your Brains for Tomorrow," *English Journal* 61:117-19 (January 1972).

Streitmatter, Kenneth D. "Student Study Patterns—A Break from Tradition," *Clearing House* 43:280-82 (January 1969).

Swenson, William G. *Guide to Minicourse/Elective Programs.* New York: Bantam Books, 1972.

Chapter 3

HOW TO DEVELOP MINICOURSES

Be not the first by whom the new are tried,
Nor yet the last to cast the old aside.
—Alexander Pope

Many schools are trying minicourse programs in one form or another. Many other schools are planning them. Still others are considering them. *How* is a school introduced to the concept? *How* does one proceed and what questions will have to be considered? This chapter will present some practical answers to each of these questions.

Stimulus to Change

Curriculum innovations, like changes in other aspects of life, come about as a response to problems immune to handy or well-worn solutions, or as the result of a widely felt need for change. Instituting a minicourse program is no different. Restless students, a dissatisfied community, anxious or adventurous teachers or administrators feel their school in need of something new and different. They hear about a successful program elsewhere and plan to institute something similar. Sources for hearing about such innovations are many—journals,* conventions, newspapers, televi-

---

*Key words in *Education Index* for references to minicourse programs include: curriculum selection, electives-short term, minicourses, elementary schools-schedules, junior high schools-schedules, high schools-schedules.

sion, and new books. Should there be an interesting program going on at a nearby school, perhaps it can be visited or the curriculum coordinator from an innovative school can be asked to visit the school wanting to make some changes.

Since the early 1970s a number of schools have felt that the introduction of curriculum alternatives was one way to deal with student unrest and disenchantment. A perennial problem, particularly in academic high schools, is "senior slump" during the spring term. An essentially community-based or service-oriented spring alternative—the classic minicourse program—has proved to be a popular way to deal with rebelliousness and boredom.

Other minicourse programs have come out of casual discussions during department meetings, particularly prior to a pending evaluation visit by an accrediting association. Such preliminary discussions are likely to begin with vague questions about a need for change and possible improvements. Then areas of specific concern emerge. Since the purpose of the accreditation visit is to stimulate self-evaluation, it is appropriate that minicourse programs evolve out of such discussions.

A common inhibitor to curriculum change is passing the buck: "But the state department won't . . ." Thus, it is heartening to learn that the modification of some state requirements has caused some schools to feel ready to explore curriculum alternatives. Another inhibitor has been college admissions requirements. But this hindrance is disappearing as colleges, particularly state universities, have modified entrance requirements to allow for the inclusion of courses that the principal of an accredited high school recommends as meeting their requirements.

A positive stimulus to instituting curriculum alternatives is outside funding. Many schools have been spurred to reshape their offerings by Title III ESEA grants. Another financial stimulus is tightened budgets. Some schools have found that instituting minicourse programs has led to a more effective and efficient distribution of limited resources.

As in any significant curriculum change, time is an important factor. When can teachers find the time to concentrate on developing new courses? Lightening the load of key teachers is one way. Selecting some to work during a summer period when they can concentrate on the new curriculum is another device.

In sum, the stimulus for developing a mini program can be initiated by reading, by visiting, by listening around, and by self-study growing out of dissatisfaction with the present situation. This dissatisfaction may be brought to a head by students, by teachers, by administrators, or by interested people outside the school. The rest of this chapter deals with ways to move the idea toward being a reality.

Organizing a Mini Curriculum

This chapter opened by citing some reasons for change and suggesting some procedures. Of course, the exact pattern and particular steps will depend upon such factors as the size and atmosphere of the school involved, the restraints or freedoms bestowed by the state education department, the readiness of faculty and community for change (students usually are ready!), and the amount of preplanning already done. A basic formula would include such factors as: determine interest, focus the response, find a teacher, publicize and explain, find a place, and find time. The melding ingredient is enthusiasm.

Administrators generally have more freedom to go to conferences and to visit other schools. Thus a principal may come back with some ideas about minicourses tried in another part of the state, after which he or she would initiate discussions with staff and students. If the idea involves consideration of electives, the usual plan is to get teachers to brainstorm and suggest courses they would like to present. Students then react to this list with a chance to add ideas of their own.

Sometimes the move to minis can be picked up from a "suggestion box" made available to members of the faculty. Among the ideas that came to the office of a principal of a Nevada high school were: Combine English III and U.S. history; broaden science 9 so that students have a choice; and slide rule instruction, horse care and training, preparing for civil service tests, parliamentary procedure, preventive maintenance, know yourself, ethnic literature, drama workshop, and Why do we act the way we do?

If the decision has been made to try some short-term courses, who should write the course descriptions? In almost all cases this becomes the responsibility of the classroom teacher—especially if this is to be a course the individual teacher is to handle. In free-form situations, which usually are heavily student-developed, students draft many of the offerings. The language arts department at a New Jersey high school blended the two contributors in this way. Members of the department wrote descriptions that tried, from *their* point of view, to make the course "salable." Then a few students were asked to come in and react to the descriptions: Are they salable from the *student* point of view? Later on, the students looked at the objectives, outlines, and resources suggested. Often they had valuable contributions to make.

Lest the teachers be pressured for time so that they blindly copy programs designed by and for another school, it pays off in the long run to provide released time during the academic year or special assignment time during the summer. While each teacher should be responsible for delineating his or her course, it is helpful to set up arrangements so that teachers can meet together to "cross-read," to share suggestions and ideas. This often leads to cooperation in exchanging ideas, materials and techniques!

Although guidelines can be stifling to very creative types, many teachers venturing into the mini field prefer to have at least a skeleton to build upon. Also this enables other cooperating planners to know what to look for and, where appropriate, to make comparative judgments.

In the initial venture, at least, it is important to inform both students and parents what the program is all about and what choices are available. People who have not had the opportunity to make curriculum decisions before should be informed and guided. In a small school the student body may be introduced to the new idea through an all-school convocation. Medium-sized schools would probably do this a grade at a time.

Eventually, however, there should be meetings with smaller groups to allow for a question and answer period. Very often this is done in English classes for two reasons: (1) English departments are usually the first to embrace the short-term elective concept, (2) English is a subject taken by all students, hence, this is an easy way to contact all of them. In some situations the guidance department has a procedure for talking with students about course selections, so counselors may be used in the information-gathering and advisory process.

Schools have a variety of means by which they can inform parents. Something really new in curriculum provides a chance to put some life into PTA meetings. Eventually written materials have to be produced. It may be a general public relations brochure that launches the venture. However, the real chance for understanding comes when the parents are called upon to participate in a decision concerning their children.

Questions to Consider

As one embarks upon a search for a different program, certain questions will come to mind. As one proceeds with one's co-workers into planning and development, some of the following questions will emerge again—perhaps from a different perspective—and new ones will occur. Just what are these commonly encountered questions, and what are some practical guides to dealing with them? Many are given below, though not necessarily in the order in which they will enter into the deliberations.

Will Students Choose Wisely?

Since the elective feature is basic to most plans and since students ordinarily have not had an opportunity of this nature before, will they choose what is "good for them"? Will they choose what looks to be a "soft" course? Will they just go where their close friends go? Will they be more influenced by who is teaching than by the topic proposed?

After the initial flurry of scarcely knowing how to handle the decision-making, most students usually do a creditable job. A few people, regardless of age (including even teachers at in-service programs) will gravitate to the "snap" course. Others choose only the most rigorous as a personal challenge. In general, as experience accumulates, the extremes level off. Students at all age and grade levels have an underground communication system. The word soon gets around as to what is worth while. A teacher, finding that few elect his or her pet course, can haughtily dismiss the situation with, "Kids are too immature to make such important decisions." Honest reflection, however, may bring the teacher to realize that although 17th-century poetry is his or her love, the adolescents' love may be Bob Dylan! Or one may discover that, although the teacher was wonderful, nobody was listening! They did not understand the teacher. "You know," one teacher declared, "it's not so much immaturity as inadequate background. Perhaps, all along the line, we should move up decision-making as an educational priority!"

While testimony from actual school experiences does not support the contention that students will always choose wisely, the majority of the schools have been pleasantly surprised. Indeed this outcome is enhanced by finding a significant increase in student motivation and interest over the previous traditional program. Students who feel that certain courses may be worthwhile will exercise their options more carefully. If none seems worthwhile, what is the difference? Speaking philosophically, if students make an unwise choice, they may profit by learning how to offset a poor decision. The school's role changes from directing students to assisting them in dealing with appropriate alternatives and their consequences.

What Grades Should Be Included?

Closely allied to trusting students maturity-to-choose is whether or not certain choices must be kept within a designated grade level or should be non-graded. By far the majority of schools, whether elementary or secondary, are moving to some degree of non-gradedness. The phrase "some degree" is included because the choices may be limited to only juniors and seniors or to the "upper division" in any school unit. This restriction is more true in academic electives than in all-school free-form experiences. Some teachers are appalled at the idea of having 15- and 18-year-olds in the same class. Yet they may also recognize that students learn from each other, not just from older adults. Also educators have long recognized that grade level is a concept based on chronological age which, unfortunately for the assumption, does not coincide with educational age or personal experience. Elementary schools are going strong for ungraded plans, but it took Frank Brown's phase-elective plan in Florida (covered in chapter two) to move secondary schools to do so.

In defense of a decision to exclude the lower division from electives, it should be pointed out that the high school has a sincere desire to see that students get a good foundation in a discipline, after which they can be allowed to make some of their own choices. It is interesting to note that schools that began cautiously, by making electives a "senior privilege," soon included juniors, then sophomores, and later the whole school had a chance to learn how to accept responsibility.*

Many schools that have expressed dissatisfaction with the tracking system have decided to experiment with non-graded electives and most are finding it satisfactory.

How Long Should the Minicourse Be?

Free-form opportunities for unassigned time may run as long as there is interest from both teachers and students. If the school is setting aside a "soul week," for example, some courses that are developmental and require continuity may meet every day all week. Other such courses may meet two or three times for a longer period during the week or for a one-time, long-block presentation.

When it comes to credit courses in the academic program, the tendency is to relate length to the marking period currently being used. Since many schools give grades on a quarterly basis, the mini offerings are thus nine or ten weeks. Ideally, the length should be determined by the nature of the topic; practically, most offerings will coincide with some administrative period. A few schools dare to present options that vary from three to 18 weeks. (See the schedule-makers tremble!)

---

*Textbook publishers are also responding to the non-graded concept. For example, Scott, Foresman and Company presents an *Index to Mini Course Materials* in which grade-level designations have been eliminated; instead the materials are "phased."

Is a Mini Too Short?

Related to the previous question of length is the concern of some teachers that anything less than a semester is too short and doesn't give teachers enough time to get to know students. This is probably true in large schools if the teacher is one who stands (or sits!) in front of the class and does most of the talking. The minicourse should be student-oriented with student participation. If this spirit is put into practice, it provides an increased opportunity to really know students, regardless of the length of time. Also, since chance for choices involves guidance, teachers are forced to look more closely at students in order to give advice. There is the thought, too, that the teacher who is actually attuned to students will have them come back in other electives.

Occasionally students will complain that they didn't have time to figure out what the teacher wanted. This may be true, if the teacher is used to wandering casually through a year course; however, when the time constraints are a few weeks, the teacher is forced to make the purpose of the course clear early on. That is why most schools require details on proposed electives. In many cases the essentials—purposes, topics, suggested activities, resources —are made available to students. A Tacoma, Washington, high school on a trimester plan with 12 weeks in each semester, has found that with their system both students and teachers are more tolerant knowing that in only 12 weeks they'll be in a new situation.

"Too short" is a relative term—dependent upon the nature of the course, the degree of student-teacher interaction, and the willingness to give it a try.

How Should One Handle the Matter of Marks?

Course grades, of course, involve the matter of failures. One plan is to offer courses on a pass/fall basis, or the less stigmatizing credit/no-credit basis. Rarely is any credit given for free-form experiences, but a notation of the "courses" taken may be placed in the individual student's file. For the one-month minicourse interim at a Wisconsin junior high school, 250 courses were offered on a pass/fail basis to remove the pressure of grades.

The minicourse program at a Nevada high school schedules a course two times a week for nine or 18 weeks. When the planners discussed an applicable grading system, they decided that either letter or pass/fail grades could be used—depending upon the request of the individual student. Credit for the class is the same as credit for other scheduled classes. The method of recording minicourses on the student's permanent record is left to the discretion of the school administration.

Pertinent to this issue is the matter of failures. If a student takes four quarters of English in a year and fails one, what grade should be assigned? An average of the four, including the failure? Some schools do this, but it is more common to let each quarter be a unit unto itself. Students must pass four quarters to get a year's credit. If they fail one quarter, they have two options: (1) repeat that course the next time it is given and hope to pass, or (2) take another quarter course. The latter option is usually taken.

What Happens to Sequences?

A common criticism of English electives is that their random nature works against the continuity necessary to build a solid curriculum. In response, one could ask: continuity of what or for whom? The subject matter? The teacher? The student? Usually most people are talking about the presumably inherent nature of a discipline: one must be able to add before one can multiply. Most traditional subjects are considered to be hierarchical in their organization so that the learner must "learn to walk before he runs." In chapter five, which looks in detail at secondary school programs, an analysis of differences in disciplines on this point will be made. Suffice it to say here that mathematics and foreign language departments are much concerned with continuity and prerequisites. Most English departments, on the other hand, are begining to see that English really isn't a sequential discipline. Some teachers realize that English is learned through impressions and the "shock of recognition." Students will learn if they are exposed to many experiences with words—reading, writing, speaking, and listening.

For a system going to a year-round program another dimension to sequencing must be considered. Each quarter (or whatever unit is basic) must be self-contained. What happens if the student elects to be absent for the third quarter? One procedure is to have subjects with prerequisite parts (as in Algebra I) offer each section each quarter.

How Can All These Courses Be Scheduled?

Almost every administrator considering multiple electives gets concerned about making suitable schedules. Will the computer be able to handle it? Can the administration afford the time and effort to "plug it in by hand?" If only one or two departments want to try quarter electives and the rest of the school is on a semester or year basis, complications can arise. Here are some different ways by which administrators have dealt with this question.

In free-form programs, the situation is less complicated once the time for the offerings is allocated. For example, at a junior high school in Santa Barbara, California, the staff decided to modify the schedule by extending the regular lunch period into two periods. While half the student body was eating, the other half was taking minicourses or getting help from teachers in academic areas at special resource centers. The scheduling was handled through the district's data processing department. Every three weeks the department sent a minicourse request card to each student, prepunched with student identification and name. This was a "sense mark" card, designed to allow all students to request two first choices and two alternate choices, and to indicate which lunch period they were taking. The list of course offerings and the marked request card were then returned to data processing. From this each student was assigned two minicourses. Twenty-four hours later the results were returned to the school, including a list by homeroom showing assignments for each student, minicourse rosters, and a course-request summary identifying courses having vacant seats. The limits established for the computer program were two course assignments per student, 100 course offerings, and a maximum of 300 seats per course.

Other opportunities for scheduling non-credit electives include: (1) suspend regular classes for a period or two once a week, (2) present the courses when a number of students have study hall or independent study time, (3) have classes meet during certain homeroom periods, before or after school, or on Saturdays, and (4) hold minicourses during the last period on Friday ("let down time").

When it comes to setting up an extensive program of short academic offerings, scheduling is crucial. Schools have been able to carry out their plans by finding a staff member who shows skill in coping with scheduling aspects for their multi-course program.

When a high school in Norfolk, Virginia, decided to put its entire school program on four nine-week divisions, it also decided to adopt a modular schedule. In this format, one-quarter credit was the basic unit of instruction and was given for a course that met for 16 modules in a six-day cycle during each nine-week period. Since six is a more versatile number than five for purposes of fractional offerings, the school operates on a six-day period of scheduling such as Monday through the following Monday. After the sixth day, the schedule repeats itself. This is a lot of new venturing for a school to undertake all at the same time, but it can work out.

A number of principals in schools offering minis in only one or two subject areas report that they went to the computer people and asked, "How can we 'cheat' on the computer to do this?" One way was to insert a pseudo-number into the listings and then "plug in" whatever minicourse seemed to be desirable at that time in terms of student selections.

A suburban Boston high school reported that they spent all summer making schedules—until they decided to imitate the college catalogue. Then their courses were scheduled and students made up their own program from what interested them and from what was available. After some "educated guesses," a simulated master schedule was fed into the computer to see what changes might be needed. The final schedule was made after two or three readings like this. Students were given four weeks in the spring to make their choices.

What is the situation in the year-round school? In their study of year-round operation, the Dade County, Florida, school district found that the "quinmester extended school-year program," by its design, required the school to develop a master schedule each nine weeks, rather than once during the year, as is the practice in a 180-day school program. The development of a master schedule each nine weeks provided a maximum of flexibility for pupil programming and made available alternatives in course selections that considerably enhanced the individualization of instruction.

A school that prefers to move cautiously might want to consider the procedure used at a suburban Washington, D.C., high school. The English option was begun with only the junior class, and the next year it was expanded to include both the new junior class and the previous year's students when they became seniors. As this is a fairly large school (about 750 in each class), it was felt that the English offerings could be broken down into enough minicourses to give all students some choice in selecting their programs. Students in both classes were assigned to a period in English. In October they were asked to make three choices each nine weeks from among the five or six courses offered during their English period. A bulletin listed the courses for the full year, by quarter, so that the students could plan ahead.

The institution of short-term courses can cause some scheduling headaches, but with a little ingenuity a school can find ways to make possible whatever seems to be educationally desirable.

What Will It Cost?

In these days of budget pinches in schools, administrators and board members will quickly wonder if a proposed alternative curriculum will cost more. Two thoughts should be kept in mind. It costs to build any worthwhile program. If a program has merit, it should be worth the cost. There is no indication that setting up a mini plan, per se, costs any more than any other curriculum innovation of equal magnitude. However, unless a school elects to stand still, it will usually find its costs increasing anyway, and a minicourse program can be absorbed into other cost increases. Given below are certain cost factors to be considered when planning electives.

The first matter relates to planning and preparation. Here the chief cost, often an indirect one, is time. If teachers are relieved of some classes to plan and write, then the hiring of substitutes

would be one item. More likely, work during the year can be absorbed during department meetings and by volunteer effort. During the summer, intensive writing is usually planned with certain
personnel hired on a time or per diem basis. Often a consultant
may be brought in during the early stages to advise and observe,
then return later to evaluate.

Does offering more courses—40 minis in the place of a few
year-long courses—mean more teachers and hence, more expense?
Not necessarily, since this is a reallocation of time. In fact, at a
New Jersey high school the English department lost a teacher
because of a budget cut. At first they feared that they would
have to cut course offerings. Instead, they turned the situation
around by going to short-term electives. Result? More courses
instead of less—even with one less teacher.

The writing of programs involves a small cost for materials,
but more expense for clerical help. Some instructional materials
will doubtless be needed, but departments that have already purchased paperbacks and corralled other supplementary materials
usually can ingeniously redistribute these in the initial year of
operation. Courses that delve into areas not usually covered, however, will naturally require a search for other resources.

Time cost shows up in some ways that are unique to short-
term courses. One was referred to earlier—more time necessary for
scheduling. Another is the additional time needed for counseling
both by certified counselors and by classroom teachers. Once
again, this is true of any venture that moves toward individualizing
the curriculum.

One aspect that should be built into any program is that of
evaluation. (See chapter six.) This calls for planning, for developing or buying appraisal instruments, for analyzing data—all of
which cost in time, and some in material.

Many schools undertaking curriculum innovations have been
able to get grants, mostly from ESEA, a few from private foundations. Thus, an elective program, instead of being an actual cost to
a school, can provide extra funding. In addition, an opportunity to
get funds can be an incentive to try something different. Two high
schools in two adjoining counties in Ohio worked together on a
joint project to restructure their curricula. This was financed by a
Title III Grant of $167,000 over a three-year period.

A free-form operation introduces other considerations of cost. Even a week once-a-year requires hours of planning time. Most ventures of this type make use of student effort; hence the demand on teachers is not so great. One bonus aspect is that many outside resource people are brought in—usually at no cost to the school. Sometimes speakers outside the immediate community are reimbursed, at least for transportation. Since many projects of this nature involve field trips, there may be transportation costs, although parents or older students sometimes help on this matter. Some courses, such as glass-blowing, may require a fee, which interested students usually pay on their own. Just as they do for a school newspaper, students may raise money for printing the program.

Ideas for Implementation

Without proper planning, any form of mini—be it free-form or academic—can become a fiasco. It can be dangerous to plunge in without careful preparation. Many schools report taking from one to two years to explore, to plan, and to propose. One of the first assessments will be to test the temper of the group concerned—especially the faculty. How far and how fast are they ready to move?

Decision-making is a good time to test assumptions. What underlines the mini concept? Whom can an innovative administrator trust for help? How much can the teachers trust the students, and vice versa? And how much can the curriculum people trust the classroom teachers? The successful operation of a minicourse program depends upon trust and mutual support.

Who will do the original planning after the idea has either been suggested or has emerged from group discussions over curriculum dissatisfactions? An administrator will need to consider whether the school or district is ready to start with a faculty-student-community committee or whether that tri-partite organization should be formed at a later time. Even if a school decides to delay the co-operative responsibility-sharing, it should get input from all groups. In the long run, someone must be given the responsibility for identifying the resources within the school—faculty, students, administrators—as well as within the community.

Most assessments of faculty readiness will find some resistance. Supervisors often comment that innovations are okay if one has innovative teachers. People are prone to drag their feet if they feel something is being forced on them. The cue here is to work with the interested teachers perhaps as a pilot study. Much foot-dragging comes from the commonest of human fears—that of the unknown: "Who else has tried it? What happened?" The material in chapters four and five might allay some fears, since it presents programs of those who have dared to try. Perhaps some key people can visit schools that have successful elective or minicourse programs.

Cautions to Be Considered

One of the best ways to calm the fear-of-change contingent is when just a part of a school or district ventures into minicourses successfully. Frank discussion about the strengths and weaknesses of an on-going program are important to underscore places where changes need to be made. Equally important is an open-minded look at proposals for and experiences with minicourses. If the schools of the "good old days" were at all successful in helping people to become critical thinkers, here is an opportunity to put that trait into actual operation. There are advantages to the mini idea; there are some shortcomings. To bring about real curriculum change, both the enthusiasts and the foot-draggers must be careful not to poo-poo the findings that do not support their views.

This book is weighted on the positive side for the mini movement, since the preponderance of reactions both in theory and in practice have been highly supportive. Consequently, a look at disadvantages and possible trouble spots is good strategy for the curriculum changer. By knowing what pitfalls may lie ahead, one can lay plans to bridge these danger spots or to route around them. Sometimes a skilled leader can turn a threat to an advantage!

In the frenzy to make the curriculum "relevant," course planners may put so much emphasis on the here-and-now that they forget the admonition, "Let no man enter here who is ignorant of the past." Today's topics are not without links to the past.

A glance at some offerings mentioned in chapters four and five will reveal minicourses that deal with the classical as well as with the contemporary, with the basics as well as with the innovations.

Another concern is that a program may get out of balance, with too many options for the independent-minded and too few reassurances for those who want to be directed by others. The plan thus should offer options for those who want to exercise a right to choose, who desire to be different. However, for those—students and teachers both—who feel more comfortable with conventional patterns, there should be the choice to remain with traditional curriculum. It is the contention of many experienced educators that gradually the traditionalists will discard some of the old once they see the virtues of the new.

Some teachers require more structure than others. If flexible and innovative teachers are chosen to undertake a pilot project, its chances of success are improved. However, if the plan involves a whole department, some teachers may be reluctant to change, and they will continue to teach mini classes the way they taught year-long classes. Students who had envisioned the minicourse as a chance to try something new will chafe under the old structure. On the other hand, some teachers may jump too far ahead of the class and wait for something to happen. To avoid these two extremes, it is important to have frequent and ready exchange among the teachers, to gauge their readiness and that of their students. Some structure and guidance while getting their feet wet will be helpful for both parties until they develop the confidence to really plunge in.

A poorly conceived course will be a poor course regardless of length. The consolation in the minicourse is that it won't have to be endured for a semester or a year! No program is a panacea for all our educational ills, but any plan that moves toward individualization has a chance of success if those behind it believe in it.

Is There the Time?

What happens to teachers who have come to depend on the security brought by several years of teaching the same two or three courses? A small town high school in New York state, after trying out quarterly elective programs in English and social studies, found that although teachers in these departments had to work harder, they were happier doing it. The course list had to be reorganized because of a switch to the quarter system. New courses had to be developed with the possibility that a teacher might have as many as 12 different courses during a year. Additional preparation time was also necessary both to examine the influx of new materials and to do research. In spite of this required added effort, the teachers responded with enthusiasm and dedication. One reason given was that they welcomed an opportunity to encounter students in areas of learning that take advantage of the teachers' training and interests.

Time is a necessary resource in curriculum development. Sometimes a money-minded school board makes self-defeating decisions. In one Connecticut high school the board reacted favorably to a department chairman's request to establish six- to eight-week minicourses. Then it refused to provide released time for teachers to prepare these courses. It is important that teachers be given the time to work out the challenges of creating short-term courses.

Will Students Attend?

The evaluation committee of one experimental free-form week reported that the average class attendance was disappointing, and even embarrassing, to the outside "teachers" brought in. Other schools have expressed concern about irregular attendance. Rather than becoming discouraged or using poor attendance as an excuse to drop the venture, a school should consider these possibilities: Were the offerings really geared to student desires? Did students have a genuinely active part in preparing the free-form week? Are students accustomed to being dragged by the nose so that they aren't ready to make and accept choices? Have the students become so motivated to work only for grades that they see no point in doing something for which no grades are given? Were the course descriptions inviting? Did students have expectations that they quickly found were not to be realized? Were the course offerings varied enough to please both students likely to report that they learned more during free-form week than in four or five weeks of regular school and to those bound to feel that it was just an in-school vacation?

These are some of the questions to be considered. Which, if any, will lurk behind a particular school's efforts to effect change will depend upon the individual situation. It should be remembered that these are cautions—not condemnations. Even an idea of high potential may face obstacles in classroom practice. The enlightened curriculum leader must anticipate problems in order to avoid them. As has been said before, "an idea that isn't dangerous is hardly worth calling an idea at all."

Basic Procedures for Designing Minicourses

The blend, recalling the curriculum stargazers of chapter one, of curriculum theory and school practice so far discussed presents a number of recurring considerations. It might be well at this point to identify the procedures that are rather fundamental in designing minicourses. The following is an outline of basic steps, which are given in the form of questions administrators should ask themselves. Most of them are self-explanatory or have been presented in the previous discussions.

1. **Clarify Curriculum Values.** Do you seek change for its own sake or out of a desire to achieve important goals that have not before been undertaken? Do you see curriculum planning as a cooperative venture involving staff, administration, students, and lay people?

2. **Choose a Basic Organizational Pattern of Curriculum.** Will you continue to look upon the educational program as a series of discrete subjects? Will you push for interdisciplinary concepts? Is there any way in which the subject matter experiences can be integrated? How far are you willing to go in developing a problem-centered program?

3. **Decide on a Staff Utilization Pattern.** In addition to decisions on who will be involved in what ways and to what extent, how will the staff operate in carrying out the program that is eventually developed? Do you vision "teams"; if so, what particular organizational type makes the most sense to you?

4. **Decide on Basic Grouping Strategies.** Will students and courses be identified on a conventional grade-level basis such as third-grade arithmetic or tenth-grade English? Will students be grouped according to ability? If so, will this "ability" be identified in terms of IQ, achievement, teacher judgment, or some combination of these and other factors? Will certain ranges, such as a three-year block of time for the upper secondary school be, in essence, "ungraded"? Will students be able to choose according to interest and, in a sense, be grouped by that factor?

5. **Identify the Target Population.** Will those entering the minicourse program be at certain grade levels? For example, in a secondary school will elective programs be open only to juniors and seniors? Will the minicourses be designed primarily for slow learners, for able learners, or for all kinds of learners? (If you use such labels, how will you determine just who these people are and what learning characteristics are to be met by the new offering?) If this is to be an experimental or pilot program, which students out of your student body will be selected for the innovative program? How will this be accomplished?

6. **Isolate the Curriculum Areas Involved.** Do you want to do a major overhaul by turning the entire school program into a minicourse operation all at once? Or do you want to select certain areas of the offerings for the initial efforts? Will this be an entire department such as English or will it be selections from that department? Will you limit any efforts primarily to the academic program or will you start out just with free-form experiences, not necessarily related to any particular discipline?

7. **Determine the Learning Outcomes.** What are the basic competencies that learners should have, if any, for entering the program? What basic competencies should be developed through the offerings? For example, will composition be built into every one of the language arts minicourses?

8. **Decide on the Options Available for Meeting These Outcomes.** Will students take required courses in exchange for being allowed to take electives? Will the minicourses be set up in certain groups from which a student must take one or more according to a prescribed distribution pattern? Might a pupil be required to take a certain course one term and then electives another? Will students be allowed to "load" their current programs with a number of electives in one field of interest?

9. **Survey Pupil Interests.** Do you intend to build a program based upon interests of students? If so, this should be implemented by consulting students at every opportunity rather than having adults speculate upon their likes and dislikes.

10. **Survey Staff Interests.** Have you considered staff interests and competence? A common approach is to have members of the staff list courses they would like to teach. This list can be presented to the students so thay can indicate their present interests and be asked to add other course topics. The blending of the interests of these two groups is the foundation for eventual course selection.

11. **Decide Upon Administrative Questions.** Shall the minicourses be three weeks, nine weeks, a semester, or some other length of time? If free-form experiences are to be tried, how long and how often will these be held? In courses for credit will they meet daily or on some other basis of frequency?

12. **Decide on the General Framework for Each Course.** Have outlines and guidelines for the courses been written? After the course offerings have been determined (either by themes, problems, skills, or topics), the written plans for each course

should include: (a) goals and objectives, (b) appropriate materials and learning activities, and (c) purposes of and procedures for evaluation.

This chapter has raised some basic questions and has provided some answers and some actual practices related to each. But where does one get the impetus to investigate the mini approaches? Testimony shows that it comes from reading, from visiting other schools, from attending a workshop or convention, from chatting with other educators. Often it emerges as a group struggles with ways to make its program more meaningful to the student body.

If the idea is intriguing, how does one organize to work out a plan and then put it into operation? The exact details depend upon the size of the school units involved, its readiness to experiment, and leadership support. A number of steps were presented in this chapter, but the basic ingredients are careful planning, hard work, enthusiasm, and cooperation.

References

Bancroft, M.A. "Scheduling for Elective Courses," *School and Community,* January 1975.

Bremer, John, and von Moschzisker, Michael. *The School Without Walls.* New York: Holt, Rinehart and Winston, 1971.

Dupuis, Victor L. "Shake-Up the Curriculum: Mini-Course Preparation." *NASSP Bulletin* 59:83-87 (September 1975).

ERS Information Aid, No. 6, "Experiment in Free-Form Education: Mini-courses." Washington, D.C.: Educational Research Service, October 1970.

Fitzgerald, Roger J. "The New Supermarket: A 'Dystopian' View of English Electives," *English Journal* 61:536-49 (April 1972).

Glines, Don. "Why Innovative Schools Don't Stay Innovative," *NASSP Bulletin* 57:1-8 (Fedruary 1973).

Havelock, Ronald C. *Planning for Innovation.* Ann Arbor: University of Michigan Press, 1971.

Heintz, Ann Christine. "Short Courses: Pathways and Pitfalls," *Media and Methods* 13:14-18 (February 1977).

Kirkton, Carole M. "A Reference Shelf for Curriculum Planning," *English Journal* 59:1306-17 (December 1970).

Meiser, Mary J. "Mini-Courses for the Self-Contained Classroom," *English Journal* 65:62-63 (December 1975).

Nott, Ronald E. "The Development and Implementation of Quarter Courses in the Secondary School," *American Secondary Education* 2:21-23 (May 1973).

Pepe, Thomas J. "Something Special: Enrichment Courses at Very Little Extra Cost," *School Management* 17-29 (April 1973).

Roberts, Arthur D., and Gable, Robert K. "The Minicourse: Where the Affective and Cognitive Meet," *Phi Delta Kappan* 54:621-23 (May 1973).

Romey, William D. "The Curriculum-Proof Teacher," *Phi Delta Kappan* 54:407-8 (February 1973).

Steirer, Michael. "English Electives Enliven English Studies," *Clearing House* 47:284-86 (January 1973).

Stern, Adele H. "Sorry, Dr. Silberman! Mini-Courses in the High School," *English Journal* 61:550-54 (April 1972).

Stum, Barnett. "Surviving Mini-Course Registration," *NASSP Bulletin* 59:99-100 (September 1975).

Weise, Donald F. "Nongrading, Electing and Phasing: Basics of Revolution for Relevance," *English Journal* 59:122-30 (January 1972).

Chapter 4

ELECTIVES IN ELEMENTARY AND MIDDLE SCHOOLS

If you want to put more "zest" in your teaching, try serendipity!*

Although the elective minicourse approach to the curriculum is mainly associated with secondary schools, today there are some promising practices in elementary and middle schools† scattered throughout the United States. Some sample offerings are sketched in this chapter.

Some elementary schools have reorganized their regular academic subjects into short-term courses—often with options for the young student. Others have set aside a day or two, or even a week, for free-wheeling, free-form tidbits. Perhaps more common is a cycle of electives, which may or may not be related to conventional subjects, whereby a part of a day, or week, or month is set aside for interest-related courses. For these, community members and sometimes high school students come in as "teachers." Minicourses are particularly useful as change-of-pace experiences at the end of the week or during the restless days of spring.

A school may want to stress a particular topic or deal with a specific problem. The minicourse as a short-term unit devised to

*This challenge comes from Ray Skinner in "Beyond Inquiry and Discovery Toward Serendipity," *American Secondary Education*, vol. 2, 4 (September 1972):33-36.

†Middle schools vary in grades involved and are included in this section since most of the examples come from the lower division of the unit involved.

be worked into the regular schedule can handle this need very well. Examples of what some specific-topic minicourses have been about are given at the end of this chapter.

It may well be that the minicourse idea has long been part of the elementary school curriculum, but under another name. During a discussion among elementary school principals, a reference was made to a mini approach in one school whereby they set aside one afternoon a week for elective "courses" in gourmet cooking and tie-dyeing. "Oh," exclaimed one of the principals, "we do that, but we call it our activity program." This may be the case in many schools, but a review of the minicourse concept as explained in chapters one and two reveals that they should be designed to offer more than the usual activity program.

The apprehension that preadolescent children are not mature enough to handle the responsibility of choosing some of their own courses, although not supported by research, is common. To deal with this, elementary schools that offer optional courses to students often ask that the parents approve their child's selection. Another deterrent to adopting minicourses is that many elementary schools have been preoccupied with other ventures such as non-graded schools, open classrooms, and individualized learning. Hence time and energy are at a premium. Rather than taking the attitude of "maybe minis later on" a school could pursue minicourses as a means to individualize instruction and to institute some non-graded classes.

Concern over sequence, continuity, and "the fundamentals" creates yet another deterrent. "How can we allow children to choose topics at random in science and mathematics?" "We have so much to do and the time is so short that we need to lay it all out in a carefully organized plan." "We have enough interruptions without taking time out for minicourses." "Parents complain too much now about our neglecting the fundamentals. We can't take more time away from them." But, continuity and fundamentals can be incorporated into a well-designed mini program, as the sample programs described in this chapter demonstrate.

Many elementary school principals and teachers have made one or another of the above objections to minicourses. Some have other reasons for not adopting them. Taken together with inertia, this reluctance provides an explanation of why the mini idea has not yet emerged significantly in elementary schools. Nevertheless, there is increasing interest in the possibilities, and a number of schools have experimented successfully with them. The following pages discuss some representative plans.

Free-Form Projects

A Classic Mini-Week

Three months of planning by the faculty went into the minicourse program at an elementary school in Virginia. Teachers were first asked "If you could teach anything you wanted, what would it be?" They responded with their favorite interests. The courses suggested by the school's teachers, and by community people, P.T.A. members, the faculty and students—including foreign exchange students—from the local high school, were presented to the students for their reactions. Eventually over 100 courses for the school's 550 students in grades three, four, five, and six were selected. With the help of their parents and teachers, the students chose which courses they felt would be most meaningful to them.

These minicourses were scheduled to meet from one to five times during the last week of April and for one to two hours daily, depending upon the nature of the subject. Each course was limited to 15, 20, or 25 students. Each pupil had a different program each day and ended the week with new interests stimulated and new hobbies begun. In addition, important liaisons between the high school and the elementary school, and between the schools and the community, were established.

There was no financial burden on the school. The expense of the many field trips included in the program (one was a trip for sixth graders to the school they would be attending the following year) were borne by individual students. The materials necessary for the courses were either brought from home, like sewing supplies, or, like fluorescent paints in "day-glo" colors, purchased individually by those pupils who needed them.

A sampling of the courses offered and descriptions of them, given below, makes it apparent that this was a very successful attempt at broadening a curriculum.

Writing Books for Children: A course taught by a local children's book author, who shared her interests and explained how she went about writing her stories.

A Look at Brazil: A brief exposure to the culture of Brazil with movies, slides, and music, both recordings and actual instruments. Also, Brazilian food, a "typical" Brazilian party, and some lessons in the Portuguese language.

An Invitation to Math: Taught by a social science analyst from the Department of Agriculture, this course led students to an exploration of symbols, shapes, change, reasoning, and patterns in mathematics. For a practical application of mathematics, students were shown how to use math on scout projects.

Glass-Blowing and Laboratory Work: An introduction to laboratory techniques as a way of satisfying one's curiosity and searching for answers to questions, emphasizing the need for accuracy and adequate record-keeping. The course also offered experience in using laboratory equipment and assistance with experiments, which concentrated on aspects of glass-blowing.

Method Acting and Interpretive Dancing: A workshop on learning how to use one's senses to pantomime and "be" anything (including a strawberry milkshake) one would like to be. Course also offered experience in creating skits and dances.

Hippy Poster Art: Making a "splash" with day-glo color and big, bold letters—a discussion of design and the execution of colorful "hippy" posters. A prize was awarded for the best effort.

Facts About Real Estate: A course in how property is sold or transferred, and what the profits of sellers and buyers are. Students also learned about monopoly and how it applies to real estate.

Pillow Making: Making decorator pillows out of two washcloths and matching thread and fringe. The course gave students something to take home and a skill they could teach to other family members.

Sportsmanship and Games: Students learned to play chess and other games both ancient and familiar, popular here and in foreign countries, for fun and for a challenge to their mathematical skills.

What's Bugging You: A course in learning to live with oneself and others. Students engaged in friendly discussions of what "bugs" people, and got help with personal problems.

One Day at a Time

The program described above is the classic mini-week that involves an entire school—students, faculty, administrators—and parts of the community. The same thing could be done on a smaller scale, either involving fewer students in the school, less time, or the same time spread out over a longer period. Such smaller scale projects also lend themselves to special ways of emphasizing their uniqueness—such as the deliberately intriguing titles given to series of "modules" offered in a small elementary school in suburban Philadelphia. These brief courses, offered to third and fourth graders on an ungraded basis, were developed by the school's principal with the help of an aide and student teachers. The courses met for a half an hour each Monday morning, with each student taking two at a time and having the option of switching one course each week. The titles of some of the courses were:

"Friends, Romans, Countrymen" (Roman Numerals)
Search and Say (Encyclopedia and Reporting)
Find Your Way (Map Reading)
The Inchworm (Measuring)
Extra! Extra! (Newspaper Writing)
Beware of the Green Ghoulies (Helping Verbs)

Another suburban elementary school developed a somewhat similar program that met for two-and-a-half hours one afternoon a week. Called "individual pursuit," the special sessions met on Tuesdays for third and fourth graders, and Thursdays for fifth and sixth graders. The program was based on assumptions common among those adopting minicourses—that even young children should be given an opportunity to choose and plan part of their educational program and that children are more enthusiastic and and productive when free to select areas of study and activities of particular interest to them. Wanting to encourage the greater degree of personal commitment that comes when students are given greater choice in what to study, teachers allowed pupils to set their own directions as much as possible and wherever practical. The school also went outside to find teachers in the community. Some of the courses offered were:

Spanish Workshop	Soccer
Antiques	Black History
Bridge	Photography
Gourmet Cooking	Silk Screening
TOPS (Take Off Pounds)	Rap Sessions

A faculty planning committee at yet another elementary school in Pennsylvania wanted their students to explore areas of interest outside the regular curriculum. By so doing, the teachers hoped to stimulate the children to develop new hobbies and expand their knowledge in a particular field of interest. They developed their series of minicourses by first asking student council members to discuss the idea in fifth and sixth-grade homerooms. The suggestions thus gathered were organized into a series of minicourses offered for three hours one Friday morning. The courses that resulted were:

Animal Study	Dissection
Mechanics	Gymnastics
Photography	Chemistry
Home Economics	Sewing, Knitting, Crocheting
ESP	Computers
Karate	Arts and Crafts
Nature Study	Rules of Sports

Several of them were taught by faculty members, community people served as instructors in others, and some were taught by students and faculty from the local high school. The program was so well received it was repeated on other mornings several times during the rest of the year.

A Program for All Elementary Grades

The school district of a college town in central Ohio developed a project, with the help of a Title III grant, they called ORBIT, for Organizing Resources by Instructional Teams. All "team" members, which included teachers, paraprofessionals, parents and other community resource people, and students in the district's schools, together researched problems or questions that emerged from the interests of one or more team members. Topics arising from students' questions were given priority. All students in grades one through eight were eligible to participate.

The project operated on an essentially integrated subject-matter basis. The primary instructional format was a problem-solving one in which the group took a large, pervasive sort of question and sought several possible alternative answers, none of which, the students quickly came to realize, was necessarily "right." Children and adults interested in some aspect of a particular problem formed a temporary task force, set individual and group goals, and studied whatever subject matter came naturally as part of dealing with the question.

The project offered several types of programs, among them (1) the inquiry center, an investigation of an open-ended question; (2) the minicourse, a rather formal presentation of a body of material; and (3) independent study, a chance to pursue personal interests related to academic areas. In addition, time was allotted for activities that might occur on a one-time-only basis, such as a special visit with someone from another country.

The following are summaries of some courses that evolved out of ORBIT's open-ended question approach. The last is one of the three minicourses developed by the project.

"How Did Language Begin?" (Grades One and Two): Children became interested in how people began to talk and how words came to be. Through the study of some Germanic words they learned of similarities between English and German. They also learned about words such as "buzz" and "gurgle" that incorporate their sound into the word itself. They became interested in dictionary meanings of their own names. The inquiry method proved to be a fascinating way to develop interest in the language arts geared to the child's level of understanding.

"What's Cookin'?" (Grades One and Two):   Children learned about nutrition, cleanliness, and foods of other countries. Activity culminated with children cooking their own lunch consisting of "pigs in blankets" and "Mickey Mouse salad" (the "pigs" were weiners rolled in biscuit dough and baked; the salad duplicated Mickey's face with pear and gumdrops). The students also learned to read recipes and follow directions.

"Moving to Music" (Grades Three and Four):   As a group of students listened to music, they learned to move as a total entity rather than as individuals. This emphasis on practice and teamwork improved their individual performances. The teamwork and cooperation also enhanced their social development and physical coordination. Their "learnings" went from split-second timing to musical knowledge.

"Architecture" (Grades Seven and Eight):   A study of house construction and the use and understanding of various blueprints in construction. The course was a combination of mathematics and social studies.

Incorporating Minicourses into the Curriculum

Free-form minicourses, particularly those not carefully planned in advance, often turn out to be one-shot affairs—successful for what they were, but not necessarily worth repeating. If the minicourse concept is to be integrated into the regular curriculum, its function for a particular school or district must be firmly decided on beforehand. The planning necessary for a mini-day or mini-week in an elementary school may seem to be too time-consuming for the special offerings to be repeated. However, modifications of the free-form approach can be incorporated into the school year—either as periodic offerings—a series of special courses that last a month or so with another series offered once or twice again during the school year—or as a cycle or sequence of short-term courses offered throughout the year. In this section we will look at some elementary plans along these lines.

A Six-Week Program

Most schools seem to go into their first mini venture on a trial basis. One elementary school in Iowa prepared a list of questions before instituting their minicourse program. The continuation of the program was to depend on positive responses to these questions:*

1. Is time taken from the regular school day justified in terms of student involvement in activities not considered purely academic?
2. Is the program acceptable to patrons in the district?
3. Are volunteer instructors prepared to meet the needs of those students choosing to enroll in their class?
4. Will students feel a sense of accomplishment at the conclusion of the program?
5. Will volunteers react in a positive way as they reflect on their experience?

The response was positive. As a result of the general satisfaction with the experiment, the school incorporated two six-week minicourse programs into their regular curriculum. They labelled their venture PEP (for Personalized Educational Participation) and offered it to all pupils on an elective basis. The faculty saw PEP as a complement to their basic program—not so much an alternate as a parallel route to helping a child's school experience come to life. Each pupil was given a chance to do his or her own "thing." Some of the courses offered during one six-week session are described briefly below.

*Courtesy of Nodland Elementary School, Sioux City, Iowa.

Bead and Pearl Jewelry: A course in which primary-grade students made their own inexpensive jewelry with materials supplied by the instructor.

Gymnastics: A course in the fundamentals of the popular art of gymnastics offered to fifth and sixth graders.

Shorthand: An introduction to beginning shorthand for fifth and sixth graders. Both boys and girls were encouraged to attend.

Model Rocketry: A course in rocketry that gave older students a chance to make model rockets using individual kits, which were provided by the instructor. The kits cost $3.00; students were also asked to bring a shoebox and bottle of white glue.

Decorating Cakes and Mints: A course in the basic steps for decorating cakes, offered to both boys and girls in grades four to six. Students brought a frosted cake to class on their day to demonstrate cake decorating.

Camp Songs: This course in learning to sing outdoor songs was open to students who enjoy vocal music in grades two through five. It was taught by a talented instructor who was also a camp counselor.

Supervised Independent Study: For students who did not wish to take part in an activity course, a room and an advisor were available to help on independent study projects.

One Month Twice a Year

An elementary school in Minneapolis set aside the month of November for a series of minicourses that met the first two periods of the day on Mondays, Wednesdays, and Thursdays. The course cycle was repeated again in the spring. Students were offered short courses in social studies, science, art, music, and industrial arts. Descriptions of some of them follow.

Masks: In this course, students explored why and where people wear masks. A combination of art and social studies, the course also gave students an opportunity to make masks of their own design.

Animal Communities: Students in this course discovered what an animal community is. Activities that were a part of the class work included tracking animals, nature hunts, and observing animals systematically. Children recorded their observations and shared their experiences.

Symmetry: A combination of art and science, this course offered students an opportunity to study things with matching parts: objects, people, flowers. Students also discovered other symmetrical objects—from buildings to butterflies—they either brought into or discussed in class.

The school also offered another type of minicourse on Friday afternoons for an hour-and-a-half period. Each week children made new choices, the selection changed from week to week. The minis offered one afternoon were: outside games, math games, marshmallow art, tissue paper art, monopoly and other games, field hockey, creative dramatics, seed pictures, jacks and checkers, and industrial arts. Most of the courses were action-oriented, designed to help pupils (and teachers!) to let off steam at the end of the week.

Six Afternoons, Three Times a Year

The sixth, seventh, and eight grade teachers at an elementary school in St. Louis met three times a year to plan a group of minicourses offered on six consecutive Friday afternoons. After the teachers drew up a list of courses they were willing to offer, the students were asked to look at the list and indicate which courses most interested them. Those with little student interest were dropped; the others were developed by the faculty member in charge. During the mini afternoons, all regular classes were suspended. Descriptions for some courses planned for one session are given below.

Crafts for the Artist: Projects planned for this course were making papier-mâché masks or banks, graphic works done with paint brushes hand-made out of yarn, and spatter prints or templates. Students were asked to complete one art project before beginning the next one.

Snow-Stuff-Acid-Tea: This minicourse on drug abuse consisted of films, group discussions, and guest speakers. One of the scheduled speakers came from a rehabilitation center for ex-addicts.

Electricity Around the House: In this course, students received a simple explanation of a house's electrical system and of how some common electrical appliances work. Students made some simple repairs—lamps, irons, switches, etc.—and learned about living safely with electricity. Students also had a chance to learn how to make their own lamps.

First Aid: What to do until the doctor arrives. This course included instruction in the 10 rules of first aid, making bandages, and caring for sprains, cuts, bruises, burns, and fractures.

Conversational German: Students learned easy German dialogue and how to sing popular German songs.

Easing into Individualization

The mini-cycle in a small New Jersey district provided elective courses meeting for a six-week period, four times a year. The courses were offered for 40 minutes Thursday afternoons, a time chosen because it was often an unproductive period. The electives at day's end on Thursday created renewed enthusiasm on the part of all. Teachers and pupils both suggested and developed courses. Topics have included "People Movers" (different types of transportation), "Bird Study," "Baton Twirling," and "Public Speaking."

The teachers and the administration in this district were concerned about the special problems their students would encounter as they moved from the traditional grade and classroom structure toward a continuous-progress curriculum. Their new program was to emphasize individualization of instruction with multi-age and multi-level grouping an important aspect. "How do we accustom young children to moving around the building?" "How do we erase the image of a particular teacher as a 'second-grade teacher'?" The minicourse program provided an answer to both questions by easing the students into individualization and multi-grade classes gradually. This was aided by acquainting students with teachers in various grades—all the teachers were seen in a broader perspective by all the students. Not only did students realize that their teachers were capable in numerous areas, they also realized that teachers, too, were people capable of enjoying many diverse activities. As one pupil said, "I know Mrs. Smith; we had fun cooking together last year!"

Easing into an Activity-Based Program

One reason often given for exploring the mini-concept is to provide a basis for formulating an activity program in a school. The purpose of such a program is to involve children in an action-oriented program keyed to each child's interest. Exposure to many different ideas and concepts through minicourses enables children to acquire a broader base for knowledge. Believing that variety enhances this exposure and is necessary for stimulation, an elementary school in Pennsylvania offered its fourth and fifth graders a minicourse program that allowed them to choose a new mini every five weeks in both social studies and science. From the course listing sent home, each child, with the help of parents, made three selections. In one period six options in science and five in social studies were offered. Descriptions of these are given below.

Chemistry: An exploration of why some important substances found in nature seem to mix together and others never do. Students performed several experiments and were encouraged to ask questions about what they were learning and had thought about.

Nature Club: The town library's membership in the National Wildlife Federation enabled the school to organize its own Ranger Rick Nature Club. Students were required to work hard in class preparing for supervised observation of nature out-of-doors, after school and on weekends.

People and the Weather: The clothes people wear, the way they feel, the things they do, the places they visit, often depend on one thing—the weather. This course looked at how man has tried to understand and predict the weather and at how the weather affects daily life.

Geography of Pennsylvania: This was a special course on the students' own state. They learned to locate it on a globe, to know its boundaries, its major cities, land forms, and mountains. They studied the weather and climate of the state and learned about similarities and differences from one part of the state to another.

It Couldn't Be Done: Feats of engineering and construction skills often inspired a great deal of skepticism prior to completion. In this course students "visited" some—the Brooklyn Bridge, the "Spirit of St. Louis," Hoover Dam, the Astrodome, and studied how the planners went about building or doing something that had not been done before. Projects in the United States were the target.

The flexibility within each minicourse, as well as within the entire program, should be designed to spotlight the individual child and his or her interests. Schools considering future possibilities for minicourses might think about offering an individual package of courses for a child who is very interested in a particular subject. Although students may repeat courses they are particularly interested in, they should be given different activities and receive new information each time.

Junior High and Middle School Programs

If the aim of the minicourse is to restructure the curriculum so that variety and choice become integral aspects of the child's experience in school, its ultimate realization is a year-long sequence of carefully designed minicourses. Two examples of such a curriculum are described below.

Junior High to Middle School to Minicourse

A number of school districts have reorganized themselves so that the junior high school is replaced by a middle school. Usually this means placing the ninth grade in the high school and incorporating the sixth grade into the new middle school unit. Administrative reorganization such as this provides an excellent chance to study curriculum reorganization. This is what was done by a small city district in Texas. A year of research and study convinced the faculty that it would be advantageous to replace the conventional curriculum with a program of minicourses. In addition, they integrated career education into all subjects in a manner that focused attention on a selected "career of the month." Some other aspects of the reorganization are given below.

Language Arts: For grade seven, three minicourses were required —grammar, reading, composition. A similar requirement was made for the eighth grade, except that only those students in the lower 25 percent of the class were required to go to the reading center. The other units were on literature, with courses based on titles chosen for their interest to students.

Science: Eighteen minicourses were devised, to be offered over a two-year period. The only required course was anatomy.

Mathematics: Because of the sequential and skill-based nature of the subject students were given a diagnostic test in order to determine their needs. This analysis occurred at the beginning of each six-week period so that students could be placed in groups with like needs.

A Comprehensive Middle-School Program

A middle school in Ohio offered its more than 500 sixth, seventh, and eighth graders a series of nine four-week-long minicourses in science. Every four weeks the students choose one of the four minicourses to be offered during the upcoming time block. A fifth option, open to each pupil, was an individual project developed cooperatively by the pupil and a supervising teacher. Through this approach the student was offered more variety than is customary in a three-year science program. Because of their concern that some continuity be maintained, the four science teachers organized the courses so they were not a collection of unrelated activities. The sum of all the minicourses and the individual student projects to be taken over the three years was designed to form a basic core of general science knowledge and concepts. An outline of how their program worked is given on page 73.

Science Minicourses Offered Each Four-Week Time Unit*

Weeks	Alternatives			
1 to 4	Introduction to Science	Introduction to Science	Introduction to Science	Introduction to Science
5 to 8	Oceanography	Insects	Microscopy	Science-Math
9 to 12	Rocks and Minerals	Photography	Plants	Simple Machines
13 to 16	Landforms	Chemistry I	Human Anatomy	Psychology
17 to 20	Insects	Chemistry II	Reproduction and Genetics	Winter Life
21 to 24	Landforms	Light	Evolution	Chemistry II
25 to 28	Rocks and Minerals	Sound	Animals	Atomic Energy
29 to 32	Oceanography	Meterology	Pollution and Conservation	Aerodynamics
33 to 36	Meterology	Camping	Ecology	Electronics

*This program was developed by the Aurora, Ohio, Middle School.

The English teachers in this same school devised their own minicourse program, one suited to the nature of their subject. Prior to the adoption of the minicourse program, each student had been assigned to an English teacher for two 45-minute periods a day. The English teachers made use of this structure by deciding to offer a traditional literature, composition, and language course during one period, and an activity-oriented project course during the other period. For the conventional English course, the program was divided into nine four-week units, just as the science department program was. Each student followed these nine units in a prescribed sequence—there were alternating units of humanities, using a thematic, literature-centered approach, and of skills, grammar, composition, and the like. In these units, the students stayed at their own grade level.

For the daily project period, the courses were ungraded and no marks were given. The courses varied in length, from four weeks to 12. Students were provided with the experience of choosing their own activities, and the necessity of accepting the consequences of their decisions. Given below is a list of titles for the project-centered courses. They indicate how an innovative program can cater to students' individual interests while maintaining continuity and control over the sum of experiences a student will be exposed to. (The courses are organized by the number of weeks each was offered for.)

Four-Week Courses

Advertising	Popular Arts
Film Study	Writing Workshop
Independent Project	Drama Workshop
Script Writing	Dialects, U.S.A.
Play Reading	Writing Poetry
Individual Reading	Writing Science Fiction
Mime and Pantomime	Photography

Eight-Week Courses

Radio Drama	Filmmaking
Slide-Tape Presentations	Television Drama
Public Speaking	Debate

Twelve-Week Courses

School Newspaper	Tutoring
Puppetry	

Instilling the fundamentals of a discipline into students is a matter of providing *contexts* for skill development. This can be done in a minicourse program by realigning priorities as exemplified by this middle-school program. Although concerned about students' need to work on their reading, writing, listening, and speaking skills, the teachers made it their first concern to design an approach that would provide meaningful opportunities for students to be *active* in their language activities, to sample a range of language activities, and to use language in a variety of situations for a variety of purposes. Hence a program with variations, but also one with continuity.

Other Minicourses for Middle Schools

Given below is a quick list of course descriptions culled from reports by middle-school curriculum people that were gathered in preparation for this book. Their subject matter and duration time indicate the amount of variety possible with minicourses. The inviting language used and the apparent practicality of most demonstrate well the ingenuity and concern teachers have put into devising these courses.

Mathematics in Sports (three weeks): Ever wanted to know how a batting average is determined? This course will show you how and teach you about other mathematics used in scoring and evaluating games, teams, and individuals in sports.

Dramatizing Mathematics (three weeks): Several skits and short plays will be rehearsed during this minicourse for presentation to other math classes. These skits will present in an entertaining fashion the need for math in everyday life.

Personal Grooming for the Summer Months (two weeks): This course will provide the basics of care of the hair, nails, feet and the rest of the body for the hot months ahead. Students will also learn basic health routines and shape-up exercises.

Successful Sitting (one month): Skilled baby-sitters are much in demand. A basic background in child care will be provided and discussed, along with suggestions for handling emergencies, feeding and entertaining children. Taking the course should enable girls (and boys) to care for children more successfully, enjoyably, and profitably.

Trimnastics (three weeks): Do you ever feel like "Betty Bounce," "Jenny Jiggle," "Sally Stomper," "Cathy Cow," or "Patty Pig"? If so sign up for this course, come down to the gym, and try to improve. No miracles are promised, but we should have fun.

Growing Up (quarter):   Having a hard time finding reading that relates to how you feel and think? Lucky you! You can sign up for this course and follow Huck, Holden, Gene, and Ralph through their difficulties as they face the trials of life and seek solutions to its problems. *Catcher in the Rye, Huckleberry Finn, A Separate Peace,* and *Lord of the Flies* will be the major works studied during this course.

How To Be the Life of the Party (one month interim):   Want to learn about what people did on winter evenings before television? This course provides an opportunity to have fun and improve one's ease at social gatherings by learning about and playing various types of house-party games. After an introduction to each game, via its historical background, participants will play games utilizing memory, rhythm, observation, and sound.

Year-Round Programs

A number of school systems are adopting or seriously considering year-round school calendars. One approach to an all-year schedule is the "quinmester," the school year divided into five equal parts. Dade County, Florida, where the plan originated, operates with a 12-month school year arranged in five blocks of nine weeks each. The plan was adopted as a solution for crowded conditions and as an opportunity to provide a greater variety of course offerings. Although quinmester plans typically begin with the secondary school, they can be adapted to elementary schools as well.

Other school systems have organized the calendar year into four equal quarters, with summer school a full quarter. Three quarters constitute the conventional school year and students have the choice of which three quarters to attend—they may stay in school during the summer and take the winter off. Most of these plans, too, are still most popular at the secondary school level, where the program is basically non-sequential, non-graded, and individualized.

Another year-round variation is the "45-15 plan," in which each student attends school for 45 school days and then has a 15-

day vacation. By staggering entrance dates, about one-fourth of the students enter every 15 school days, the first group to enter completes its 45 days of learning and starts its vacation the day the fourth group enrolls. This plan, for which a minicourse approach is particularly appropriate, has been adopted by some elementary schools.

Regardless of what form the plan takes, these or some other variations, they do mean that the elementary teacher will have to consider the implications of facing a new group of students at each new block of the school year. The school itself has to consider what happens to course sequence. The development of self-contained, short-term "courses" is one solution.

The Jefferson County, Kentucky, school system is one of the few that offered an all-year program to its entire student body, from first grade through high school. For elementary schools, adapting the notion of continuous progress to a year-round program cut up into quarters that all students do not attend consecutively presented obvious difficulties. One solution was base the curriculum on levels rather than quarters because levels are tied to students and not to calendars. The Jefferson County schools attacked the problem by taking a K-12 view in curriculum planning. A master design provided an outline giving a recommended sequence for skill development, major concepts and skills for each quarter, and then aided teachers in designing suitable minicourses for that quarter.

In order to come to grips with what could and should be taught in any quarter, the Science/Social Studies Writing Committee for grade three in the Jefferson County schools sent an evaluation form to each elementary school principal. The principals were asked to meet with all third-year teachers to discuss the results of teaching from a preliminary draft of the master design during the fall quarter. Each teacher was asked to check those suggested activities that were successful in the classroom and those that needed to be explained more fully or revised in some way. They were encouraged to describe any procedures or ideas they felt would strengthen the courses: was the course too long, too short, or just right?

Reorganization of the school calendar demands a reorganization of the curriculum. When this happens in an elementary school, it provides a chance to study mini approaches to programs for young children.

Other Uses for Minicourses

Specific Topics

Some elementary schools find that their students would benefit from studying a particular topic. Instead of trying to incorporate these topics into existing courses (to which they relate) a special course can be planned. The course can be designed for whatever length seems appropriate and a convenient time slot for the students taking it can be selected. Thus an elementary school in suburban Philadelphia introduced a pilot course on "anti-smoking." It met for a 50-minute period once a week for six weeks, for pupils in grades four, five, and six. A modified course on the same topic was presented to the primary grades. The course was based on the assumption that students should "stop before they start." One result was that many children went home and tried to get their parents to stop smoking.

Another specific minicourse in the same school district offered to sixth graders was called "the money tree" and dealt with consumer concerns. Federal funds obtained through the state home economics department underwrote 90 percent of the cost of the program. A former home economics teacher came in once every two weeks for a total of 10 class periods. In this course, the sixth graders were introduced to the importance of establishing monetary values and of making wise decisions in the market place.

Another school district adopted the minicourse approach to a career-guidance sequence for students from kindergarten through high school. The courses were part of the social studies program. Classroom teachers were asked to develop individual-learner units designed to be bridges from the sub-concept level to behavioral objectives and suitable activities. Each individual-learner unit (teachers in the district developed over 1100 units at various levels, K-12) had an objective that required pupils to consider which careers or occupations they might want to pursue. Among the objectives for the elementary schools were (1) assisting the children develop an understanding about themselves, their values, and an appreciation for all types of work and (2) developing the emotional as well as the cognitive growth of the individual. The occupations and careers were grouped into 10 major clusters. As each grade level was introduced to a predetermined number of these career clusters, a block of time (approximately two days) was programmed for the corresponding activities, which were handled in the form of a minicourse.

Minis for the Gifted

Although there are many books and countless articles that deal with the education of the gifted, there seem to be few minicourse programs specifically designed for them—which is unfortunate as well as surprising, since the enrichment offered in minicourses is particularly appropriate for unusually able children. The Memphis school system is an exception to this. Through Project CLUE (Concerned Leadership for Urban Education) they established seminar classes wherein academically talented students from grades four, five, and six spent one morning and one afternoon each week. The seminars were begun after the system took a serious look at what it was doing for its gifted students. They devised a minicourse program that consisted of six to eight lessons and challenged the children to learn something about psychology, archaeology, etymology, anthropology, logic, and the heart and circulatory system. The reaction of students and parents to this program was overwhelmingly favorable.

Because gifted children are able to assume a great deal of responsibility for what they are learning, grade-level designations are often unnecessary. Because the gifted are often interested in many things, or intensely interested in one or two things, it is possible to give them a great deal of latitude in picking the structure and content for their courses. The minicourse, with its intensive, short-term nature, is particularly appropriate for these students.

Fostering a Relationship between Elementary and Secondary Schools

Minicourses can also serve to improve articulation between the elementary and the secondary school. A brief exposure to a variety of subjects can help students in middle schools or junior highs decide on what electives they want to take in high school. Further, able high school students can be asked to teach small groups of elementary or middle-school students, which is just what was done in a foreign language program at a middle school in Tennessee. During two 20-minute periods each week, the sixth-grade pupils participated in a minicourse in French, Spanish, or German. Each course ran for four weeks, and concentrated on vocabulary and culture. They were all taught by two carefully selected high school students who worked each class as a team.

A School within a School

Called "society school" or "children's university," an experimental school can be set up within an elementary school. The inner-school can be devised to perform certain functions—either for some students all the time or for all students some of the time. The separate school can serve either slow or particularly able students with courses devised especially for them. Such a society school set up in a Manhattan public school was, in effect, a simulated society which aimed to provide meaningful incentives for reluctant learners.

"Children's university" might be the name given to such a one-afternoon-a-week program. Conceived of as a miniature university, a program like this provides an excellent vehicle for offering minicourses. Courses can be written to read like a university catalog—architecture, physics, law, writing. During the latter part of the term, when the weather improves, a switch might be made to outdoor activities including physical education and handicrafts projects. One very successful such "university" course is a tutorial —in this case a course in which an above average student helps those having difficulties. The possibilities with this as a framework are endless.

All of these elementary and middle school ventures show cautious moves on the part of teachers and administrators to grant children the experience of learning how to make choices and to live with the consequences of their decisions. As the principal of a middle school once noted, the minicourse approach to curriculum can change the attitude of students toward themselves and toward schooling.

Some elementary schools have reorganized their conventional academic subjects into a variety of short-term courses with options for their young students. Perhaps the most common is a cycle of electives, which may or may not be related to conventional subjects, whereby a part of the school week is set aside for interest-related courses. Such endeavors usually involve community members as some of the teachers—further enhancing the school-community relationship.

These various plans strengthen the "basics" by placing them in situations where their importance is enhanced by student interest and variety. In addition, topics, problems, and areas of learning not found in the usual program are made available. The total effort is curriculum expanding and augurs well for the future.

Meanwhile, what is going on in the secondary school? Chapter five will present some dimensions and descriptions.

References

Beers, R.B. "Use of Activity Centered Minicourses to Solve Difficult Educational Problems," Science Teacher 40:26-29 (September 1973).

Casey, Lyner, and Greevy, Pat. "Primary Options: A Decision-Making Program for Children," *Momentum* 6:16-19 (February 1975).

Dyer, Daniel. "An Alternative for the Middle Years: English for Little Big Men," *English Journal* 60:1091-94 (February 1971).

Findley, Carol. "Implementing Mini Programs for Middle School Gifted Students." ED 109 846 (ERIC Microfiche).

Foster, Lillian. "The Outside World Is In," *Saturday Review,* 24 June 1972.

Friggens, Paul. "New Impetus for the Year-Round School," *Readers Digest,* March 1972, pp. 115-18.

Kratzner, Roland, and Mannies, Nancy. "Individualized Learning for Middle School Pupils," *Clearing House* 47:280-83 (January 1973).

Madison, John P. "Innovations and the Elementary School Curriculum," *Elementary English* 49:434-43 (March 1972).

Musso, Barbara B. "Micro Resource Units and Substitute Teachers," *Education* 90:16-17 (September-October 1969).

NASSP Spotlight. "New Curriculum Stimulates Middle School Students," January 1977.

Valley View Public Schools, Research Office. "Feasibility Study of the 45-15 Plan for the Year Round Operation of a Public High School Served by an Elementary District Already on the 45-15 Plan." Romeoville, Illinois.

Chapter 5

MINICOURSES IN SECONDARY SCHOOLS

*A mistake is evidence that someone has tried to do
something.*   *—Andrew Mellon*

Secondary schools all across the country are experimenting with
courses of varying lengths. Of the five major academic areas—
English, social studies, foreign languages, science, mathematics—
the first two have seen the most activity. Short-term innovations
are also found in home economics, art and music, physical education, health and recreation, and industrial arts. Examples of
minicourses from these various fields are given in this chapter.
They illustrate the diversity of offerings as well as their range in
length—from one day to one semester.

Of particular significance is the content of these short-term
electives. Curriculum planners find them an effective way to re-
spond directly to the many concerns of the adolescent. The inherent flexibility of the mini permits the quick discarding of
courses that no longer make sense to the learner as well as the
rapid development of new courses to deal with the changing scene.

Students who graduate from a high school that has tried
minis should have learned something about deciding between alternatives and also have had chances to explore topics of personal
concern, both opportunities not available in many high schools.

Since the minicourse is relatively new, mistakes in implementing them have been made. Adjustments take place, but few
schools that have tried minicourses have abandoned the idea com-
pletely. In general, experience with minicourses at the secondary
school level has been satisfying—for students, teachers, and par-

ents. Why this is so will be examined in the following pages, with descriptions of both representative and unique courses. The discussion will center on two aspects of adopting minicourses: (1) what is going on in traditional subject areas and (2) what courses on special topics or themes are being offered. The latter courses, such as ecology, are sometimes found in one department, sometimes in another. Often they are given as an interdepartmental course.

English

It is appropriate to begin the presentation with offerings in English.* Almost every high school that has considered going into short-term, academic electives began with English courses. For those few schools that started with other departments, the English department joined quickly.

The broad goals of any good English program are to help learners think, speak, listen, read, and write to the limit of their capacities. Probably no secondary school, independent or public, would disagree with these goals, but how are minicourses providing opportunities for students to do exactly those things? Most minicourse proposals stress vocabulary development and writing skills. Nearly all expect basic reading skills. If a student's reading ability is considered to be poor, or needing special development, there are reading electives available. To a degree, minicourses can remove the stigma of needing special help—if all students have elective courses, students needing remedial work won't feel singled out.

Requirements for Basic Competence

Should the electives be open to all? In spite of the recognition that English offerings need change, variation and a new look,

*For a detailed discussion of English electives see the chapter "Course Offerings" in George Hillocks, Jr., *Alternatives in English: A Critical Appraisal of Elective Programs.* (Urbana: National Council of Teachers of English, 1972).

in most four-year high schools, there is some reluctance to extend the opportunity of taking electives to ninth graders. The rationalizations include: (1) freshmen are not ready to make choices; (2) teachers need a year to get to know students' strengths and weaknesses so that they can intelligently advise them when they are ready to choose; (3) there are still certain basics that teachers must be sure students have; (4) students may be entering the high school from different schools and hence may lack a common foundation.

The distribution of courses is also a matter of concern. With 50 options, John may choose only literature, while Mary will try to get just writing courses. Consequently, many schools require that the electives must be in different areas. A regional high school in New Hampshire limits its elective English to grades 10, 11, and 12. Students are required to take (and pass!) at least a semester of writing, American literature, world literature, and self-expression prior to graduation. A three-year Connecticut high school offers both 10-and 20-week electives. The English distribution requirement is that all students must elect 12 quarters of English during their three years. These courses are to be divided as follows:

Three quarters in writing courses
Three quarters in literature courses
One quarter in spoken arts courses
One quarter in other language skill courses
Four quarters of free electives

The matter of requirements is an attempt to insure basic skills as well as to provide a balance among the choices. At an intermediate high school in western Pennsylvania, freshmen and sophomore students are considered non-graded and are required to develop minimum communication skills through both an individualized program called learning activity packets and group instruction. After students demonstrate the desired grasp of skills, they move into nine-week minicourses. If after extensive testing a student still shows a deficiency in basic language arts, composition, and speech skills, the English department reserves the right to schedule the student, at its own discretion, into a course or courses designed to improve basic proficiency.

The course listings that follow are borrowed directly from school catalogs. Those selected from the hundreds available show the variety possible. Notice the attempts at "salesmanship" through titillating titles and provocative descriptions. In some cases prerequisities are listed, but most courses are non-graded and self-contained. The duration given for each course was standardized for the purposes of this listing. The time indicated in parentheses following the course title assumes that the course will meet three to five days a week for the time given—in weeks, quarters, or semesters. Any prerequisites are given in parentheses following the course description. Especially important in all of these course descriptions is the recognition of the interests, concerns, and needs of today's youth they express. Some school catalogs give, after each course description, a line titled "benefits to students." Including such a line is an excellent public relations gesture, particularly if the lists are sent home with students. Such a line, of course, need not be included, but thinking of each course in terms of what the student will "get out of it" is a useful exercise which might prevent a school's offering a lot of idle fancy under the guise of the minicourse.

English Fundamentals

English Workshop (quarter):   This course is designed for those students who have difficulty with the basic aspects of reading, writing, and speaking. It is definitely not recommended for college-prep students. Only students whose diagnostic tests indicate problems may sign up for this course.

Everything You Always Wanted to Know about Reading but Were Afraid to Ask (quarter): This course is designed for students who are articulate and capable of critical thought but are hampered by slow reading and poor spelling. This course will include word attack exercises, spelling generalizations, drill, and vocabulary study in order to help the students improve their language skills. The course will also include literary analysis through listening to records and reading shorter works of major writers. Admission to this course is by approval only.

Listening (three weeks):   This course aims to develop listening as a *skill*. The listening skill will be treated as a complex composite of many factors: hearing acuity, auditory perception, purpose, attitude, attention, experience, and training. Students will receive specific training and will participate in listening experiences to demonstrate skill with the kinds of listening: (1) purposeful accurate listening, (2) critical listening, (3) appreciative listening, (4) creative listening. A tape-recorded series *Listen: Hear* will be one of the many devices used. Special effort will be made to reinforce all training in order to stabilize listening skills.

Morphology (three weeks):   Sounds scientific? Well, it is. The study of the structure and forms of words is a science and a very practical one. Participation in this course can lead to improved spelling, richer vocabulary, and more correct word usage. After all, if one knows how a word is made, one is well on the way to mastery of its use.

How to Speak (one month):   "Mini-Toastmasters" is a course designed to increase effectiveness and confidence in public speaking. Skills will be developed through conversations, readings, televising, tape-recording, discussions, and demonstrations.

English Lab (quarter):   This course is to be offered only to students who have been pre-tested and found to read at the fourth- to sixth-grade level. It will emphasize the four communication skills: speaking, listening, reading, and writing. The course is designed to help the students compensate for an inability to read and write through an intensified program of oral-aural communication skill building. Skills to be developed include:

Listening:	To follow detailed directions and instructions.
Speaking:	To correct everyday errors of non-standard usage through patterned oral drills.
Reading:	Development of vocabulary and comprehension of expressed language.
Writing:	Sentence sense through usage rather than by grammatical approach; legibility of handwriting, composition of simple sentence patterns, paragraphs, and poems.

Countdown: Language Arts and the Turned-Off Student (one month): Open to any student, this course is primarily designed for students too long accustomed to frustration in English. Students will read mysteries, sports articles, and jokes, write directions for a map and learn secret codes while they build up map-reading skills, and learn to skim, spot topic sentences, and group facts. (Prerequisite: Recommendation of counselor.)

Literature

Introduction to the Novel (semester): Here's an opportunity to read selected best sellers for pleasure and credit! If you've always been terrified of the "novel," this course will calm your fears by introducing you to some of the most exciting and meaningful literature ever written. After an introductory analysis of the genre, the course allows for study of representative works ranging from English standards to Mario Puzo's *The Godfather*. (Prerequisite: Junior or senior status.)

Knights of the Frontier (quarter): What kind of people tamed our frontiers? This course will study the pioneers, explorers, mountain men, Indians, gold seekers, and others who expanded America's frontiers. Students will read books and magazines, fiction and non-fiction, to determine the character of these "idols." *My Life as an Indian, A Woman of the People, Shane, The Way West,* and others will be the texts.

A House Divided: A Humanistic View of the Civil War (quarter): The tragedy of the conflict that pitted man against friend, brother, father, or son will be studied through works approaching the Civil War from a humanistic viewpoint. Films and recordings will be compared to the original literature by Margaret Mitchell, Stephen Crane, Stephen Vincent Benét, Walt Whitman, Ambrose Bierce, and others. (Prerequisite: Tenth-grade reading level.)

The Devil in Literature (quarter): This will be a great course for students who have always been fascinated by camp stories about ghosts, goblins, witches, and the Devil. It will include reading stories by Poe, Chekhov, Milton, Jackson, and Hawthorne.

Shakespeare Sampler (quarter):   To gain an appreciation of the versatility of Shakespeare, the class will read a tragedy, a comedy, an historical play, and some of the sonnets.

Perusing Periodicals (three weeks):   Through examination and discussion of selected periodicals, students will develop a clearer understanding of important issues, advertising propaganda, present-day humor, and opportunities for jobs. This course will acquaint the student with the importance of the periodical in America as a source of information and leisure reading. Some time will be devoted to a discussion of such early periodicals as the *Saturday Evening Post*. The student will read such current periodicals as *Time, Newsweek, Readers Digest, Ebony,* and magazines published for readers with special interests such as *Popular Science, Popular Mechanics,* and *Modern Photography*. Students will write simple accounts of what they have read.

Author Search (quarter):   This course offers students an opportunity to concentrate on an American author of interest to them. The class will stress independent study techniques and methods of sharing in-depth information on a variety of authors. Students will study a number of works by a single writer of their choice (novelist, poet, short story writer, biographer, literary critic, and other non-fiction writers).

Poetry Specials

20th Century British and American Poetry (quarter):   Through the poetry of T.S. Eliot, Robert Frost, William Carlos Williams, and Wallace Stevens, the progressive alienation of modern man from traditional values and institutions will be traced. A return to and reaffirmation of some of these values will be studied in the works of local and contemporary poets.

English Q Sound and Sense (semester):   This course will emphasize the importance of sound to the development of meaning in poetry. Time will be given to those students who are interested in writing poetry. The basic function of the course will be an attempt to create and cultivate a "poetic view."

The Rock Poets and Their Dads (quarter): This will be a comprehensive study of many of the modern poets who not only write poetry but sing also. It will include a close scrutinization of the works of the Beatles, especially of John Lennon and Paul McCartney as rock-philosophers. Some other poets to be studied are Donovan, Rod McKuen, Kahlil Gibran, and Janis Joplin. These poets will be compared to their predecessors and contemporaries, E.E. Cummings, Thomas Hardy, Langston Hughes, Countee Cullen. While the main emphasis in this unit will be on the basic philosophical tenets evident in all poetry, it will also include a study of rhyme, rhythm, meter, alliteration, metaphor, etc.

Topics and Themes

Literature of Sports (quarter): This course will involve a study of novels, short stories, magazine articles, and poetry that have sport as their subject and/or setting. Emphasis will be on literature of quality (Malamud's *The Natural* and Harris's *Bang the Drum Slowly)* and not merely on popular sports, books, and magazines. All works will be examined with regard to theme, structure, and style. Through the course, students' ability and interest in reading should improve.

The Photo-Essay (quarter): The photo-essay is here to stay. With big glossy photographs and bold captions and texts, book publishers, popular magazines, and even newspapers have turned to the photo-essay as a way to tell a story. Students who have a camera and film will have a chance to make their own essay. Take a look at the world!

Love American Style (quarter): Is there anyone beyond the age of 10 who has never said, "I love . . . "? It is unlikely. We are inundated with TV ads telling us how we will love a perfume, a car, a piece of furniture, a beer, and even a deodorant. Is this love, or a misuse of the term? In this unit we will look at this much-used term and attempt to arrive at an understanding of "that which makes the world go 'round."

Women and Liberation (trimester): Students will determine the direction of this course, possible selections are Kate Millet's *Sex-*

ual Politics, Germaine Greer's *The Female Eunuch,* Simone de Beauvoir's *The Second Sex,* and Betty Friedan's *The Feminine Mystique.*

The Fine Art of Dating (one month): A coeducational course for ninth graders offering guidelines for making it easier to achieve poise in the dating game. Experience and knowledge in the rituals of dating and dining out, of conversation, introductions, etc., will help make good manners come more naturally.

Vision of the Future (three weeks): What will the world be like in the future? Students will seek answers to the question by reading what famous journalists and other writers have said. How one adapts to change will also be included.

An Ordinary English Class (quarter): This course is for students who "sorta" miss English the way it used to be. One week we may be studying composition, the next a little poetry, and the following week we may read a novel. It is the little of everything that is supposed to be English. In some ways it's a mystery course—the curriculum will depend on the class and the teacher. The only thing required is that it will be an English class like those we had before we adopted quarter courses.

Social Studies

Many of the basic concerns discussed in detail in regard to English electives could be repeated for social studies and for the other disciplines reviewed in this chapter. Is sequence necessary? Perhaps, but it should be recognized that adolescents will have been exposed to a chronological course pattern prior to high school.

State requirements? As with English, a certain number of years (varying in each state) is mandated. In social studies the requirements usually include a year of American history and government, and sometimes the government of the particular state as well. The common practice with a mini approach is to offer a number of electives dealing with the American heritage and then declare that x number of electives from this group will satisfy the state requirements.

There is attention to fundamentals in that much reading is usually involved, so reading, note-taking, and writing are of concern. Some schools include a mini on "how to study." The following are catalog descriptions of sample courses which have been instituted in schools around the country in the hope of removing the apathy—even the antagonism—toward social studies. These courses show not only variety, but also a willingness to delve into areas not usually included in a regular curriculum.

Mission Possible—Self Instruction (quarter): The purpose of this course is to introduce students to the written resources available in our high school, both in the library and elsewhere. Students will be taught to locate and organize information in a logical and intelligent manner.

Psychology (quarter): What is an inferiority complex? What do daydreams and unnatural fears mean? This course may not cure anyone of these or other conditions, but it will help students learn more about their own personalities and why human beings behave as they do in adjusting to a complex world.

Seminar on R. Buckminster Fuller, or How To Use Your Dome (quarter): An intimate seminar of 10 students committed to intensive reading, writing, and discussion of the thought and practice of R. Buckminster Fuller: "A comprehensive, all purpose, long distance, world-around genius talker who teaches everything to everyone everywhere . . ." In one great leap, Fuller has crossed the generation gap and has taken the young with him on a trip through the universe. Fuller traces man's intellectual evolution and copes with some of the great problems we face today: How is man to survive? How does automation affect the individual? Where are we to find resources to feed the poor? This course will acquaint students with Fuller as an "explorer in comprehensive, anticipatory design science."

Life in the 1980s (quarter): Will students have to wear gas masks to school in the future? Or maybe drive cars that float on air? Will long hair styles give way to crew cuts? These and other questions will be asked and discussed in trying to find out what it will be like to live in the 1980s.

Advice and Consent (quarter): The intricacies and interrelation-ships of the branches of our federal government and the various agencies and departments therein are the focus of study in this course. A detailed review of some of the points of interest and precedent-setting events that have occurred in the relations be-tween particular presidents and the Congress will form the core of the course.

The World Is Your Oyster (quarter): A geography course without specific assigned readings, without textbooks, formal assignments, or tests. Classtime will be mostly allotted to travel movies and slides, and very short (five minute) lectures. Students are to plan a dream trip overseas (outside North America). Plans shall be de-tailed.

The Film and You (quarter): This course is intended to be a mind-expanding experience. The best in short-length films will be viewed and discussed to see what we see. No attempt will be made to establish similar opinions; rather the student will be encouraged to enjoy the film for whatever personal pleasure it may bring. To better accomplish this end, the art of film-making will be studied by the student as part of a small group that will be responsible for producing its own film. The course will be conducted in two parts: the first, the study of the film in seminar; the second, a workshop in creativity.

Is God Dead? (quarter): "There is no one alive today who knows enough to say with confidence whether one religion has been greater than all others." This course will cover the origins of reli-gions taught in the West, primitive religions, paganism, witchcraft, as well as a study of Judaism, Roman Catholicism and Eastern Orthodoxy, and Protestantism. The course does not include and is not intended for use as religious instruction. Its content is fac-tual and objective. Local leaders from each of the three major Western faiths will be invited to take part in the course.

Europe Today (quarter): Plan an itinerary for a trip to Europe! We are in a period of time when travel is rapidly becoming a vital part of our educational experiences. Each student will select five European nations to tour through research. We will study how to get passports, proper immunizations, the best ways to travel from the United States, also how to travel in countries to be visited, their customs, and money, and other items of interest relevant to the countries we plan to visit.

Social Studies Seminar in Curriculum Development (quarter): This multi-purpose course is open to all students with an interest in determining what, how, and why we study the social sciences. The course is by nature experimental and therefore flexible. Students will be asked to select, prepare, and present a model of a social studies course they feel should be incorporated into the school curriculum; or, students will be asked to devise a method of evaluating the social studies courses already offered in the schools in terms of student-determined criteria. The key to the course is a student-determined analysis of what we have, are, and should be doing in the social studies.

Mathematics

An examination of the literature, as well as of school catalogs, reveals very few minis in mathematics. Dealing with the inherent sequence of the discipline is a fundamental problem. If the year of Algebra I (Geometry I) is cut into quarters, each would be a prerequisite to the next, and the student usually would not have the option of taking any quarter at any time. However, there are some alternatives, as the following examples illustrate.

If a school system plans to adopt a year-round program, then each quarter must be self-contained. Even though the quarter courses may have prerequisites, the mathematics department will have to examine carefully its traditional program. As they considered a school year organization based on a year-round program, district planners in an Iowa city noted some pertinent questions for mathematics teachers to ask themselves. These questions,* which any mathematics department might well ask of itself, include:

*Developed by the mathematics department in the Cedar Rapids Community School District, Iowa.

1. Prior to the school-year reorganization, how many different individual class preparations did you need to make? How many do you now make? Do you feel that the preparations you now have are creating the positive results that the reorganization was intended to achieve?

2. How essential is your math sequencing? How many courses do you offer that do not require a prerequisite? Has your reorganization made your math curriculum too segmented (fragmented)? Has the enrollment increased or decreased in courses requiring a prerequisite?

3. Do you have a geometry course? Is it sequenced? When is it usually taken? Does a skills course precede each course so that a student "failing" the skills doesn't get into a course he or she is destined to fail in? How many incoming sophomores end up in an "advanced" math course their senior year?

4. Initially, how was the sequencing, if any, achieved? Were the courses revised so that teachers felt they weren't accomplishing as much as they had prior to the reorganization? How did a teacher decide what to exclude from the "normal" course of study?

5. How many math courses are offered for the non-college-bound? How many math courses are offered for the non-math-oriented? How many math courses are offered for the college-bound?

6. Is extensive pre-testing done so that a student may "pass out" of parts of a sequence?

Schools contemplating an overhaul of their mathematics program might find it helpful to diagram the possible paths students can take through the curriculum. The chart given on the following page illustrates one such plan. Considerations such as those indicated by the chart have led to the creation of short-term mathematics courses, descriptions of which follow the chart. (Note that some have sequence prerequisites, others do not.)

Suggested Pathways in Mathematics

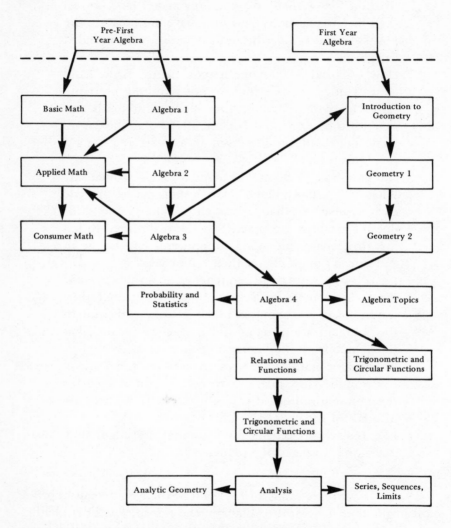

— Courses shown above dotted line are taken in Grade 9.

Courses shown below dotted line are offered in senior high.

— Follow arrows to the choices, or once you are as far as you want to go or can go, you may retrace your pathway and follow a new one.

This chart provided through the courtesy of the John F. Kennedy Senior High School, Cedar Rapids, Iowa.

Applied Algebra (quarter): Civil service tests, apprenticeship tests, and exams used by industries all include math sections. Applied Algebra will help students cope with advanced vocation-related mathematics problems that can be solved with a knowledge of algebra. (Prerequisite: Introductory Algebra II.)

Informal Geometry (quarter): This is a course designed for those students who desire a short general exposure to some of the important aspects of geometry. Also, students not sure of their desire to take geometry may want to take this course as a preliminary to a full year of geometry. Informal geometry will concentrate more on the practical applications of geometry than on the abstract, although some abstractions will be presented. Hopefully, the course will supply incentive for more advanced work not only in geometry but in other related courses. (Suggested prerequisite: General math or equivalent.)

Economic Survival (four weeks): Students will learn the basic mathematics that relate directly to their daily affairs and future personal needs. Topics to be explored include: "Cars, Who Needs Them?," "Banks, Don't Rob Them, Use Them," and "The Best Buy in Town." Problem-solving will be emphasized in developing understanding as well as skills. (Prerequisite: Mathematical skills applications.)

Mathematics Reading (seven weeks): This open-ended course may be taken in lieu of or in addition to any enriched mathematics course by superior students. The course will consist of reading and conferences on an individual basis. (Prerequisite: Permission of department chairman.)

Mathematical Oddities (one week): This course is designed to explore mathematical oddities both fascinating and useful, but outside the usual mathematics curriculum. Topics will include: pathological curves, curves without tangents, curves without length, curves that fill area or space, Moebius bands, Klein bottles, and other unusual surfaces; inside and outside; knots and links. (Prerequisite: Senior status.)

Unusual Measurements (one month): During this course, students will examine a variety of practical measuring instruments and techniques. Science and mathematics equipment will be used. Emphasis will be placed on measurements seldom tried out by junior high students.

Cultural Implications of Mathematics (semester): This course is designed to explore some of the influences that mathematics has had on science, religion, philosophy, and the arts. The contributions made by individual mathematicians will also be considered. Topics will be limited to permit in-depth study. (Prerequisite: Interest in mathematics and history.)

Introduction to Computer Programming (one month): An introduction to the BASIC language and the fundamental concepts of programming. Students will be involved in writing and executing programs.

Catch-Up Math (quarter): This course will review some of the basic arithmetic students need in shop work and help them become familiar with arithmetical operations necessary for solving practical problems in shops. It will consist of laboratory experiments using simple machines and instruments to stress the mathematical aspects of problem-solving. Individual instruction programs will be worked out.

Mathematics for Carpenters: (one semester): Recommended for students with credit in general or basic mathematics who are interested in relating mathematics to building problems. The course consists of a review and application of arithmetic operations. It will deal with volume and area measurements and everyday problems in the building trades.

Automotive Mathematics (quarter): This course will explore the mathematics of all aspects of automobile ownership. Purchasing, financing, maintenance costs, and the mathematics of automobile mechanics are some of the topics to be covered.

Genius? Genius! (one month): Have you ever had an idea that someone laughed at? If so, you can appreciate the frustration that some of our great thinkers have encountered. Meet some of these in our great mathematicians, and learn about and work with some of their contributions to society.

Logic (quarter): This course begins with a study of sets and relations carried through "truth tables." Logical connectives and proofs will be covered, concluding with symbolic sentences. This course is simply the algebra or math of computer programming with extensions.

Sciences

A review of the science offerings in most secondary schools indicates four conventional titles—general science, biology, chemistry, and physics. Basic, applied, and advanced courses within each of these are often offered, but rarely are many short-term elective courses on aspects of them offered. Need this be the case? Sequences within each branch are deemed important and are thought to preclude an elective approach. But look at the rather standard list of goals for a science program given below.

— Background in as many areas of science as possible
— Development of scientific attitudes
— An appreciation of science in everyday living
— An understanding of technological developments
— Development of inquiry skills
— Development of problem-solving ability

Do these necessarily require year-long, locked-in courses?

Some secondary schools have successfully revised their science curriculum by instituting a variety of quarter courses. These are offered in a carefully devised sequence that allows students a choice of courses and a chance to get the prerequisites necessary. Students in programs such as this are advised to carefully select their science courses, basing their choices on their educational and vocational aspirations. One freshmen science program at an innovative high school in rural Illinois offers 11 units, each nine weeks long. All students are required to take a course entitled "Metric System, Map, and Time" and then choose any three from the remaining 10 units. These are:

Space Science	Weathering and Erosion
Ecology	Oceanography

Elements and Radioactivity   Heat and Light
Rocks and Minerals   Force and Motion
Meteorology   Electrical Energy

Most science programs offer these topics in one course or another, but providing them as options is not so common. Course descriptions from programs in other schools are given below.

Environmental Studies (one month): This course is a series of 18 sessions which cover various topics of environmental stress such as people, wildlife conservation, noise, air, water and thermal pollution. Class members will be afforded an opportunity not only to participate in the sessions but also to investigate one or more of these topics on an independent study basis.

The Mini-World (three weeks): This is a course devoted to microbiology. Various samples, such as pond water, will be studied microscopically and ecological relations will be discussed and applied to our own environment.

Consumer Chemistry (quarter): This is a laboratory course in which household products are analyzed. Materials to be studied include soaps and detergents, vitamin C in fruit juices, aspirin in pain killers, and the chemicals in bowl cleaners and bleaches. Various brands will be compared experimentally to determine which is the "best buy" in terms of cost of active ingredient.

Radiochemistry (quarter): An introduction to radioactive isotopes for interested students and for those who plan a career in the medical field. The course explains the nature of radioactivity and makes use of instruments to detect and measure radiation. There will be two periods of discussion per week and three periods of laboratory work on chemistry projects.

Agricultural Science (one month): This course presents an overview of the seven generally recognized areas of agriculture: agronomy, animal, poultry and dairy husbandry, horticulture, ornamental horticulture, and food industry. The topics covered (landscaping, crop production, food industry) are designed to acquaint the student with agriculture and the effect it has on the consumer. (Prerequisite: Recommendation of counselor.)

Ideas and Investigation in Biology (one month): This course, for students who want to spend most of biology class time in lab, contains five basic units, each of which develops a "great idea" of science through individualized laboratory investigations. The great ideas include: ways in which man discovers more about his natural world, how life changes through time, how inherited characteristics are passed from generation to generation, balance in nature, and how living things react with each other and with their environment.

Gardening (one month): What do plants need to grow? Questions like this will be answered while students observe plants growing in terrariums and mini-hothouses. Planning a garden will be part of the course.

From Boone to Bag Limits (one month): This is a course for modern woodspeople. The early portion of the course will cover a brief history of the American wilderness, and some of the men, women, and legends that have shaped American attitudes towards the out-of-doors. The main body of the course will concern itself with habits of game animals and techniques of hunting and trapping, hopefully developing a sense of oneness with wild things.

Tidal Pools (one month):   A study of pools left by the tides, the formation of the pools, the organisms they contain and their importance in marine study.

Modern Foreign Languages

Modern foreign language, as much as any other subject area, has been affected by external circumstances. The anti-Teutonic feelings aroused by World War I caused German to practically disappear from secondary schools. Other language enrollments declined throughout the first half of the 20th century until Sputnik in 1957 spurred Congress to pass the National Defense Education Act. One aspect of this legislation was to stimulate foreign language instruction. Federal money for equipment and materials revived many a foreign language department. In the last decade, however, the blight of "urbanitus" and student concern for "relevance" have been taking their toll on interest in foreign languages. Courses in French, Spanish, and German are scarce indeed in schools serving low-income families. With high schools dropping knowledge of a foreign language as a graduation requirement, and colleges not requiring one for admission, the interest in offering them has again declined. Some schools have tried to buck this trend by instituting a variety of language courses designed to attract students, particularly with courses that concentrate on the people and the culture rather than on verb form.

Through a Title I grant some schools in Minneapolis established a foreign language mini-program—two-week summer sessions of saturation with French. The program was essentially made up of 10 short dialogues based on situations appropriate to summer life: "Greetings," "Giving Directions," "At the Kiosque," "Table Conversations." In addition, teachers in the greater Minneapolis-St. Paul area and in St. Louis, as well as in other large urban centers, have developed short courses on topics that seem to be of interest to students. Because of scheduling difficulties, many foreign language departments offer these minicourses as electives *within* a foreign language class. However, some are offering quarter courses or interim-period experiences with other foreign languages. One popular notion is an introductory course that allows freshmen to sample several foreign languages before being asked to commit themselves to the study of any one language. Some schools have found this a way to reverse declining enrollments in foreign languages. A real mini-mini was offered at a high school in Connecticut, a state with a large Italian-American population. The course was called "So you Want to Learn Italian . . . in Three Days!" The assumption was that by learning a certain number of basic words, phrases, and expressions, students would gain an interest in the language and the culture.

The German department in a California high school developed 44 courses under an individualized learning plan. To facilitate scheduling, students registered only for "German" and the particular course pursued was determined and recorded by the department itself. Specific behavioral objectives for each course, unit, and assignment in German were given in the student materials themselves. Students were evaluated individually after each assignment. Evaluation was based on the learner objectives with a high performance criteria. Sixteen assignments or "hours" of work, evaluated at 90 percent achievement or more, was the minimum amount of work for earning one unit of credit toward high school graduation. An assignment or "hour" of work was determined by the past experience of teachers; they decided what could reasonably be expected of the average student if he or she made diligent effort for at least one hour. Students received credit only for having learned this amount of material, however, and not for having "served" a specific amount of time.

While a number of language courses are semester length, many also allow for individual variation, as noted in the following course listings.

German for Commerce and Business (quarter): Designed for those students who might be interested in the possibility of preparing for the business world in such areas as import-export, working for American firms who do business with Germany, American firms in Germany, and the German business world. Also, special vocabulary for those interested in short-term employment in Germany, such as working in hotels or resorts, in agriculture, and so on.

The Russians Are Coming (one month interim): Common conversational phrases dealing with a variety of topics will be taught. Russian folk songs and folk dances will be interspersed with learning to write the Russian alphabet. A field trip to the Russian section of a city is a possibility, so that students may observe at firsthand aspects of the Russian culture that will be discussed in class.

Aprende Una Nueva Cancion (two weeks): This unit teaches students to sing a song ("Chile Lindo") in Spanish and to learn something of Chilean culture. The course includes learning guitar chords and instruction in playing simple Spanish songs.

Espanolito (three weeks): This course is designed to give students "a little bit of Spanish" with simple, easy to understand basics of the Spanish language. It includes the skills of comprehension, pronunciation, speaking, and reading, "Espanolito" also consists of learning about the cultures of Spanish-speaking countries. The materials used consist of tapes, records, filmstrips, classroom objects, and a Spanish periodical. (Students already enrolled in Spanish are to sign up for other minicourses.)

French Cooking (one month): A lunch-time course open to French students in grades 9-12. Preparation of French dishes combined with French conversation held in a home kitchen. Included will be crêpes, quiches, omelettes, coq au vin, and desserts. Students will be asked to pay for groceries.

Making French Come Alive (quarter): A course in which the students share their creativity with others in writing a script for a French play, acting it out, making costumes, and filming or presenting it. A course in which the student will actively exercise the skills of oral communication, reading, and writing.

Other Course Possibilities

The five subject areas investigated so far are the backbone of most secondary school programs. Since English, social studies, mathematics, science, and foreign languages are conventional subject areas of long-standing reputation, and geared to college preparation, they might not be expected to present optional programs. Nevertheless, many departments do offer lively and solid options and so the discussion often has been in detail. The next section looks at how the mini-concept has been picked up by program offerings other than the "big five."

Home Economics

Families in Crisis (quarter): This course is for students who wish to consider social and world problems as they involve the family unit. Topics for study include: new forms of family living such as communes, pollution, over-population, drugs, alcoholism, divorce, death, mental illness, and money problems. (Prerequisite: Junior or senior status.)

Bachelor in the Kitchen (quarter): A minicourse to acquaint boys with techniques used in preparing appetizing food. Laboratory experience, simple menu planning, cooking terminology, and meals for entertaining are included. (Prerequisite: Senior status.)

Supermarketing and Appliance Cookery (quarter): In supermarketing emphasis is placed on budget shopping and familiarity with federal food and drug regulations. Information on the selection and care of large and small equipment is also discussed. Opportunity is provided for the student to present a food demonstration. (Prerequisitie: Foods.)

Industrial Arts

Big Brother Program (semester): This course is designed to provide experiences for high school boys, recommended by their counselor, who would enjoy teaching and working with younger boys (junior high). "Big Brothers" will assume a wide variety of responsibilities, which might range from putting together and issuing materials, machine repair, making teaching aids for giving individual instruction, and demonstrating their use.

Cost Estimate (semester): Do you think you will ever own a home? Well, if the answer is yes, you might be interested in this course. It deals with estimating the cost of construction for a home from the ground up. Students will be required to contact local contractors and suppliers to estimate costs. There will be various areas which you will study about cost estimating.

Something New From Something Old (one month interim): A short course in refinishing furniture, picture frames, or decorative objects of wood. Search your attic for pieces that can be restored. Then learn how to remove old finishes, prepare the surface, and refinish, using such techniques as distressing and antiquing.

"Dear Charles Atlas—I've Taken Your Course, Please Send Me My Muscle" (three weeks): This course, to be offered when favorable weather conditions allow activity out of doors, is designed to teach the student how to construct weights and other body-building equipment inexpensively, using pipe, cans, rope, and concrete. The first week or so will be devoted to construction. Then students will learn the value of body building for athletics as well as for daily life. The mechanics, advantages, and disadvantages of weight lifting will be covered while using the equipment the student has made. Students to furnish as much of the material as possible and will pay whatever costs are incurred using school material.

Art and Music

Art Appreciation (quarter): Slides, film strips, and field trips will be used to emphasize the relationship of the artist to his particular culture, the influence of technological discoveries on artists, the significance of painting, sculpture, architecture, and other art forms in the stream of history. Course will cover prehistoric period through the Renaissance. Not a lecture-test course; verbal ability strongly recommended. Evaluation will be based almost entirely on class participation in discussion and seminar groups. (Prerequisite: Average to above average reading ability.)

"Do Your Own Thing" (three weeks): This is a course to give the students an opportunity to experiment with art media of their choice and understand how all things that we see and do come out of a person's creative act. Emphasis is placed on the individual's development in the use of specific art forms. The student who wants to develop initiative, self-discovery, aptitudes, individual achievement, self-confidence, release of tensions, personality, balanced living, and appreciation for life should take this course. If you are an individual who wants to learn to communicate experience, feelings, and ideas, develop natural creative ability through the uses of color, line, shape, and texture effectively, you should take this course. Students will develop their ability to use their senses to solve problems.

Pseudo-Porcelain, Alias Bread Dough Art (one month interim): In 20 days there were created roses and snails, daisies and bugs, mushrooms and elves, and a house with rugs. These are only a few of the interesting and unusual items that can be made from "pseudo porcelain," a combination of bread dough, glue, and food coloring.

Bookbinding (one month interim): Make your own scrapbooks, sketch books, photograph albums, and such. You will be doing everything from cutting the paper for the pages to designing the cover.

Experimental Music (six weeks): A course in which any group of musicians can get together and play jazz, blues, rock, folk, soul, and classical music. Students will write and create their own compositions.

Art and Music of the 20th Century (six weeks): An exploration of art and music from Picasso and Stravinsky to avant-grade electronics and group sculptures. Emphasis will be on how each development reflects the tastes, values, and problems of the society from which it comes.

Through History on Strings (one month interim): Enjoy folk music. Many folk songs have played an important part in the history of the United States. The melody and lyrics will be learned and analyzed in relation to the period of history in which they were written. Students must have their own guitars.

Physical Education, Health, and Recreation

In some schools the physical education courses are set up on alternating four- and two-week units. For example, archery, flag football, tennis, and camping might start the first month. For the following two weeks, electives might be horseshoes, gun safety, weight training, and speedball. Other short-term elective courses are described below.

Venereal Disease (one week): A frank and down-to-earth discussion of the subject. The course will basically consist of lectures and discussions.

Spelunking (one day): During the first two hours, the course will be an orientation to the fundamentals of spelunking. During the afternoon session, the class will take a hike through a nearby cave. First session mandatory for afternoon trip.

Officiating (one month): Football, field hockey, basketball, wrestling, baseball, softball! Do you like sports? If so, here is a course that will sharpen your knowledge in the rules of a variety of competitive activities. This class will prepare you to become a P.I.A.A. rated official, and in so doing, you will be able to continue with an active interest in your favorite sport. In order to complete the requirements of this course, you will be expected to participate in practical game experiences. (Prerequisite: Junior or senior status.)

Outdoor S.P.A.C.E.S. (one week): This course is for seniors interested in developing outdoor skills and applying these in ecological field studies of the Puget Sound area. These field studies will include overnight camping trips on Puget Sound, at Mt. Rainier, and on the Washington coast. This will be a full-time offering; participants will not have time to take other courses. A laboratory fee of $20 will be required for meals and expenses on field trips. For information and application form, see counselors.*

Inter-Disciplinary Opportunities

American Studies

Education Through Inquiry (full year): This course on American thought will be a study of the United States through the art, literature, and music of the different time periods. Each period will be explored through a different discipline. Cultural and social change will be studied by these different means. The course, which meets two periods per day, is structured in a two-period block of time and combines what was U.S. history and 11th grade English. The class will be team-taught with two teachers. Materials will be multi-media: print, films, audio tapes, etc. Subject matter will stress vocational application and interest of the students enrolled. The history will be covered by topics and English will be used in connection with reinforcing this material.

*Though this course is obviously appropriate only to a Seattle-area high school, similar courses using local natural resources could be devised.

The American Character (quarter): The course will be team-taught by members of the social studies and English departments. It will concentrate on the student's discovering the nature of what it's like to be American. Materials from many disciplines will be used, including art, literature, music, and history.

Writings That Have Shaped Government (quarter): This is an English and social studies interdisciplinary course, with anticipated team teaching shared by instructors from the two departments. Beginning with Plato and continuing through Karl Marx, theories of government will be examined through authors such as John Locke, Montesquieu, Thomas Jefferson, James Madison, Woodrow Wilson; and documents such as the Magna Carta, the Declaration of Independence, the United States Constitution, and the United Nations Charter. Each student will be expected to acquire some knowledge of each author, theory, and document and to take part in oral and written assignments based upon the reading. Students may elect either a social studies or an English credit for this course.

The Arts

Contemporary American Culture (quarter): This is a student-structured course that will be taught by a team of teachers from the art, music, and social studies departments. It will allow students a wide latitude to pick and choose one area of study. For example, one could study family life in American society or the youth subculture, its music, art, literature, and morality. Students will work as individuals in small groups and large, with time given in class to present their work to the whole group. In the end, each student will be asked to evaluate our society to determine what is fad and what is permanent. At least four weeks will be spent on a study of modern music and art.

Music and Poetry (six weeks): This course will attempt to give the student an understanding and appreciation of music and poetry as correlative art forms. The similarities and differences of music and poetry will be examined. This course will be audio oriented and involve listening to various recordings and tapes. The student need not have had any previous musical knowledge or background.

Topics and Themes of Concern to Adolescents

An Adolesent Odyssey (quarter): Growing up was never easy. The dominant theme of many novels is an adolescent's struggle to become an adult. The search for identity made by four young fictional characters will be the foundation of this course. A comparison of their problems and their solutions to the problems of present day adolescents will be explored. Readings will include *To Kill A Mockingbird, The Red Badge of Courage, A Separate Peace,* and *Catcher in the Rye.*

Starting With Eve (six weeks): This course will trace the impact of famous women on their age and on history. Many outside speakers have been invited. Attitudes and changes in them will be discussed.

Body Talk (quarter): Are you aware of your other self? Why don't more men like to dance? Are football players more responsive than musicians? This will be an informal experience-oriented unit in which students are directed through a series of exercises designed to give them a greater awareness of their own bodies and those of others. What is it like to be blind? Deaf? Quadraplegic? Crippled? Dumb? While some materials will be available like Joy and Yoga manuals, most of the class time will be devoted to working out situations and life experiences with the entire group. This course is for open-minded students interested in discovering how the body communicates, often without the person's knowing it.

Paradoxes, Fallacies, and A Swindle or Two (six weeks): Subtle errors in reasoning, as well as hard-to-accept conclusions obtained by correct reasoning, are endlessly fascinating and often intellectually significant. Examples for discussion and argument will come mostly from philosophy, logic, mathematics, and science. (Prerequisite: Senior status.)

Who Am I? (quarter): This course deals with situations we all must cope with throughout our lives, personally and socially. Such aspects of life as loneliness, anger, sex and love, choices, crime, getting by, happiness, drugs, and friendship are some of the feelings we will explore. (Prerequisite: Junior status.)

Careers

Look at Yourself and Careers (two weeks): This course, under the direction of the guidance department, will include interest, aptitude, and personality testing. We will have group discussions about career decisions and opportunities.

You and Your Future (quarter): This is a course that offers a number of opportunities for career-minded students who want to establish some direction for their future. What careers will most need workers in coming years? What college or vocational school offers the best training for a particular career? These questions and others will be answered through student investigation, class speakers, interviews and meetings with the guidance department and the state employment commission. Basic skills in writing letters of application, in arranging personal interviews, and in vocabulary development will be emphasized. Students will be required to keep a journal relating to the above materials and to write a detailed paper concerning their selected vocations—its future trends, work conditions, requirements, and general advantages and disadvantages.

Why Education? (quarter): Interested in teaching? Then why not find out what Socrates and others have said about educating mankind. What has changed since you started school? What were schools like for your parents and grandparents? Where is education going? Activities will include research, discussion, and field work. Evaluation will be determined by the group.

Math Aide (quarter): This course is open only to students who have been approved by an individual teacher in the mathematics department. The student will become that teacher's aide. The duties and responsibilities will be determined by the teacher in charge. These duties will include tutoring, grading papers, preparing assignments and tests, and other mathematics projects. The course may be taken until the desired amount of credit is earned.

Community Classroom Coordination (one month):   Community classrooms and career electives are an effort to provide meaning- ful, stimulating, innovative learning experiences that will enhance both the student's educational experience and the climate of the community. Seniors, faculty advisors, and community sponsors will work together to structure challenging programs that allow for an exploration of subject areas not available in the traditional school curriculum. The goals of the career elective program are directed toward self-realization and self-discovery through self- initated projects.

The minicourse movement has had its greatest impact on the cur- riculum of secondary schools throughout the United States. The impetus generally comes from the English department. Vaughan and Curtis* explain the elective emergence in English as "to avoid the limited scope of traditional programs which had emphasized narrow behaviors such as isolated skills and factual recall." Cer- tainly a review of the selections reported in this chapter indicate increased scope, great variety, functional utilization of knowledges and skills, and cognizance of that ephemeral phrase "meeting the needs of students."

Secondary school philosophies usually indicate support for the belief that people are different. This should include the con- cept that both teachers and students vary in backgrounds, in abilities and in interests. Why shouldn't courses vary to reflect these differences? Secondary school leaders have responded by developing free-form offerings, by utilizing so-called free periods of students, by cooperatively planning courses varying in length from a few weeks to a full semester, by instituting some interim efforts to bring about a change of pace. Most academic fields be- come involved with the quarter system being the most common.

How does all this effort and activity turn out? Chapter six will show how assessments have been made and what the findings have been.

*Joseph L. Vaughan, Jr., and Sherry Curtis, "Evaluating a Thematic-Elective English Curriculum." See ERIC ED 101 375.

References

Bolinger, Dwight. "Let's Change Our Base of Operations," *Modern Language Journal* 55:148-56 (March 1971).

"EJ Elective Catalogue: A Directory of Mini Courses and Electives," *English Journal* 64:55-83 (January 1975).

English Journal. Issue of April 1976.

Gordon, Judith. "Avoiding the Grab-Bag Curriculum: An Attempt at a Structured Elective Program." ED 087 040 (ERIC Microfiche).

Hach, Clarence W. "Needed: Sequences in Composition," *English Journal* 57:69-78 (January 1975).

Harley, Marvin C., and Hoy, Wayne K. " 'Openness' of School Climate and Alienation of High School Students," *California Journal of Educational Research* 23:17-24 (January 1972).

Hillocks, George, Jr. *Alternatives in English: A Critical Appraisal of Elective Programs.* Urbana: National Council of Teachers of English, 1972.

Jackson, Dorothy J. "Process Verification of a Career Counseling Program." ED 124 862 (ERIC Microfiche).

Miceli, Connie. "Minicourse on Careers," *Science Teacher* 41:38 (January 1974).

O'Donnell, Holly. "Quo Vadis Literature," *English Journal* 66:94-95 (February 1977).

Potts, V., and Kemper, R. "Micro-Mini Units for Junior High School," *Clearing House* 48:530-32 (May 1974).

Rallo, John A. "A Cooperative French Program: A New Approach," *Foreign Language Annals* 2:474-76 (May 1969).

Sheffield, Walter R., and Elliot, H. Hays. "A Microteaching Project at Fairview High School," *American Secondary Education* 3:45-46 (December 1972).

Skolnik, Herman "The Relevancy of Science Curriculums to Professional Careers in Industry," *Journal of Chemical Education* 48:566-68 (September 1971).

Vaughan, Joseph L., Jr., and Curtis, Sherry. "Evaluating a Thematic-Elective English Curriculum." ED 101 375 (ERIC Microfiche).

Chapter 6

EVALUATING MINICOURSE PROGRAMS

Not to go back is somewhat to advance
And men must walk at least before they dance.
—Alexander Pope

Evaluation is an integral part of curriculum improvement. Planning for any type of course takes time and effort. Even if the result is a one-day mini, interested teachers and students have had to spend countless hours to organize it properly, to arrange for "teachers," to get students registered, and to have locations available. Is it worth it? The consensus is "Yes," though there are some dissentions and disappointments as in any new program. Important goals —students' renewed interest in school, learning to accept responsibility, and a revitalized curriculum—are often part of program descriptions. Were these goals reached? This chapter will look at this and related questions to see what answers have been obtained and how appraisals have been made.

In view of the importance that curriculum theorists place on evaluation, it is discouraging to find that evaluation is neglected in many mini undertakings. In surveying programs for this book, letters were sent to schools and school systems throughout the country. One of the questions asked was "What is the reaction of students, teachers, and parents to this alternative?" Another question asked was "Have you made any systematic evaluation yet?"

To the first question, most schools replied that they had received some kind of feedback. As one principal noted, "Our staff and students have received this program very well, and we were extremely pleased with our initial program last year." However, almost no school did what its leadership considered a "systematic evaluation." A typical answer to the second question was: "We have made no formal evaluation. In the first year, the minicourses were given a favorable report, so we moved further into the program." Somewhat disconcerting was the reaction, "Well, this is only the second year of our plan, so we haven't had time for any evaluation yet." Evaluation, as a force in curriculum improvement, should precede, be concurrent with, and follow any curriculum innovation.

Feedback as Evaluation

The most common method for making program appraisals is to get reactions from the chief participants—the students and teachers. Sometimes this reaction-gathering is very informal. At a department meeting a teacher might report: "The kids seemed to like it. Two or three asked if we could try some different electives next year." A more systematic way to evaluate is through the use of a questionnaire to elicit and record reactions. More and more schools seek student opinions as well as teacher judgments. Increasingly, parents are also asked for their opinions.

Reactions to Free-Form Programs

Several dimensions of the free-form experiment were evident in the analysis an elementary school in Virginia made of its free-form week. Many resource people from the area participated, and all the adults said that they really enjoyed the teaching. Many new interests were stimulated among the students and several hobbies emerged. Since elementary-secondary articulation is desirable, the cooperation with high school students helped establish a better understanding between them and the younger pupils. The pupils themselves commented that it was fun to have different teachers; the teachers, for their part, were "surprised and happy" to see how well the groups of different age and grade levels worked together. (This last observation serves as a tip for administrators who seek to interest their faculty in multi-age, non-graded classes.)

After free-form week, the administration solicited statements from students and teachers, including both staff and volunteers. What "messages" should a curriculum developer find in the following comments?

— "Free-form week was real fun because you can choose your own subjects and you don't have to be told what to do or what class to go to."

— "I think free-form week was the best thing we did this whole year."

— "I taught in a kindergarten class. I liked them and they liked me."

— "I learned a lot I didn't know from free-form week. I wish it could have lasted longer."

— "Such a tremendously successful week! As a teacher, it was by far the most exciting program I have participated in. I thoroughly enjoyed it. The children liked the variety of experiences, field trips, and being aides in the school. They want free-form week every year."

An Indiana high school that established free-form week as their answer to the challenge of experimentation had a carefully developed and systematic appraisal plan. Their forward-looking view was indicated by the fact that the original proposal to the school board stated that formal evaluative procedures would be implemented upon the completion of the minicourse activities. They used three different questionnaires. One was administered only to a limited sample—those students and faculty members who were involved in planning the program. The second and third questionnaires were given to all students and instructional personnel who participated in the program. One was designed to gather data relative to the total program, a general evaluation. The third questionnaire sought reactions to each individual course offering. All three questionnaires were administered and collected the same day. Some of the responses they received were:

— "Learned more this week than in four or five weeks of regular school."

— "We hope we'll have this every year because it gives students the break they need before school is out."

As far as individual courses were concerned, the reactions were generally favorable. However, an analysis of the comments indicated that in a number of cases, revisions were desirable in course content or teaching method and that changes in teacher assignments were needed in some cases. The majority of the students felt that their participation was a good educational experience.

The conclusions made by the evaluation committee underlined the fact that planning even for a week is a tremendous venture. However, the total experience challenged teaching methods and traditional curriculum offerings and inspired the implementation of the "paper philosophy" of pupil needs and interests. Their conclusions may serve as cautions to others.

Parent Perceptions

Principles of learning suggest that what a person perceives as important is important, at least to the individual involved. Parent contributions are utilized in most free-form programs and in non-credit sessions (especially at the elementary school level). Sometimes parents are instructors in a class. Sometimes they are resource people. Sometimes they bring in equipment or help with transportation for field trips. Even if they are not direct participants, they are interested in what is happening to their children. Are they as enthusiastic as their offspring seem to be? Do they feel that a minicourse is an unwarranted usurpation of time away from "schooling"? What do they think about breaking year-long courses into quarter segments? Do they like to have their young people given freedom to choose from a number of alternatives?

A program for gifted students devised a questionnaire that was sent to parents. It provides a guide to what other schools should ask of their mini programs. Parents were asked if their child had:

— Developed an interest in subjects not taught in regular school?
— Shown a greater interest in the world around him or her?

— Developed a better attitude about his or her ability?
— Benefited a great deal from the program?
— Shown an improvement in thinking ability?
— Indicated a definite dislike for the program?
— Developed organizational ability?

When an elementary school in Pennsylvania elicited reactions from its parents concerning their minicourse program in science and social studies, they received these comments:

— "Bill has really gotten involved with his minicourses and, as a by-product, has learned through practice how to go about preparing a report with a fair amount of ease."

— "Time seems so pleased with the minicourses and all the new things he is learning. I feel they have made a big difference in his school day and are the greatest thing to come along. Keep up the good work!"

— "The entire family has learned much from these courses at dinner table discussion. The rocks and minerals topic has always been Steve's hobby and our basement has a sign reading 'Wilson's Lapidary Museum.' With Steve's enthusiasm, and the new oceanograwhly topic, I envision myself scuba diving this summer on some desolate island. Keep up the good work!"

— "Lisa has been very excited about the minicourses. I think she enjoys being able to choose the courses and then gets very excited about the various reports and information she must obtain for her papers. She bubbles with such enthusiasm that she shares with us at the dinner table all the daily information obtained at class sessions and so we are learning with her."

Some schools moving to a quarter plan seek to provide opportunities for more contacts with parents. One procedure has been to invite parents to participate in small group sessions focusing on school procedures, curriculum development, and the new school-year schedule. This way school leaders can get direct feed-back without having to prepare a questionnaire. Curriculum change, to be effective, requires the support of parents. Support depends upon understanding, which is enhanced by good communication.

When an innovative private school begins to look at itself, it wants to know whether or not both student and parent reactions are positive. If there are 500 children in the school and 700 on a waiting list, they can be fairly certain that they are doing a good job. If those parents who have children in the school already report that their children like school better, that there is less hassle getting them up in the morning and off to school, they have another indirect sign of assent.

Other Feedback

Although a principle of minis is to allow students electives, these electives do not come about willy-nilly. Counselors play an increasingly important role in helping their charges make decisions that they will want to live with. Teachers in a department offering minis, for example, try to work closely with counselors to see that the courses are personalized. At the same time counselors have a responsibility to assist students in choosing appropriate courses and in gathering feedback for the various departments. A good counselor should see to it that students have an opportunity to become diversified in their course selections and that students take advantage of the opportunity.

An Ohio high school measured the success of its elective English phases by four criteria—statistics supplied by counselors, the comments and evaluations of the students, the number of other school districts that contacted it about its program, and the success and progress of the graduates from the elective program. In this school, 35 percent of the students were electing to take more than the required four years of English. In some cases this was because the students recognized that they had certain academic shortcomings and they could use an extra elective to strengthen their pre-college or pre-job background. That more than half of the new elective courses had never been offered before was seen as evidence that other students, too, sought to enrich themselves. As one non-college-bound student told his counselor, "Nobody ever let us dumb kids write poetry and plays and stuff for a grade before."

Most schools have learned the importance of a proper attitude on the part of the teachers. Change may be especially painful for experienced teachers. It may be interpreted as "I'm wrong." When the feedback reveals criticism of the mini format, it is important to look behind the reported criticism to see if the objection is actually a cover-up for something else. Offering many courses in place of a few with students able to select may mean that a teacher's pet course has to be discarded. Teachers with seniority may have become used to teaching only two different courses—and to top sections. Now they may have several new courses to prepare and teach each quarter—to students that come from several grades and ability levels. No wonder teachers find flaws in the new. Will the feedback revealing student enthusiasm for the new courses help open up their attitude and change resistance to acceptance? Teacher attitude change will facilitate the implementation of curriculum change.

External Evaluation

An outside agency sometimes stimulates the development of new programs, and sometimes serves as an appraiser of a plan already under way. Many secondary schools throughout the country belong to one of the regional accreditation associations. Visiting teams from these associations can do an "outside" evaluation, which may be more objective than when a district or school does one on its own. Such an evaluation will at least provide a different point of view.

For example, when planning for an evaluation visit, high school departments usually spend much time looking at themselves in terms of items in the evaluative criteria.* A review of the statistical data gathered on the student body and the community should help members recognize the nature of community

*One of the most widely used forms is the *Evaluative Criteria* of the National Study of School Evaluation.

—and hence student—changes. This, in turn, could motivate consideration of how a department might institute changes to increase the effectiveness of its offerings in view of the fact that its student body is different than it was a decade earlier. One result in several schools has been the development of minicourses to provide more timely topics at varying levels of difficulty.

When a North Central visiting committee took a look at the English program in a high school in Missouri, they made several recommendations. Prominent among them was the suggestion that students should become involved in developing the curriculum as a means of making their education more relevant and viable. They also suggested that students should be provided outlets for their creativity. One result was the development of a minicourse sequence for a three-week interim in January as a pilot project. The reaction of students, teachers, and parents to the project seemed to be supportive. To test this assumption, the English department circulated to students a questionnaire which included the question: "Would you like more minicourses throughout the year?" "Yes" was the response from 89 percent of those students who responded. As a result of the accreditation-stimulated desire to involve students in curriculum planning and the feedback from participants in the pilot programs, minicourses were instituted as a part of the program of studies in all three high schools in the district.

Another external evaluation device is that of bringing in education consultants to assess the success and impact of current instructional programs. This may be particularly effective for a small district with few if any complicated problems. A very small rural school district in Alaska asked two university professors to come look at their new program, which they did by systematically interviewing approximately half of the students in the elementary and secondary schools and all the teachers, teacher-aides, and community minicourse teachers. The interviewers also sought parents' perceptions of how the new program was working. The questions revolved around student interest in school, the minicourse concept, academic *vs.* vocational courses, student freedom, required courses, competency of staff, college preparation, and an exchange travel program.

Parents in general indicated that they were pleased that the new plan gave students a lot of opportunity for different kinds of experiences. Almost all the interviewees felt that the pupils were adjusting well to the program and its "openness." From all the comments reported, only a few were negative and these dealt with personalities, with lack of notice of coming events, and with the complaint that "There isn't enough homework."

Measuring Student Progress

Achievement

Parents may be pleased that their children find short-term electives "a lot more exciting," but these parents also ask, "Yes, but are they achieving?" To answer this question, an Ohio high school prepared graphic achievement records every nine weeks for the students who participated in their English pilot program. The graphs charted individual student scores in English (from the Ohio Survey Test), letter grades in English for previous years beginning with the eighth grade, and letter grades in the English pilot program. An analysis of the achievement graph of an individual student enabled a teacher to observe whether or not the student was working up to ability and whether or not this had changed with the student's participation in the pilot program.

From individual graphs, a composite graph was made for each grade level in an atempt to present a visual representation of the accomplishments of the program. The English department, upon studying the results, concluded that "the pilot program achieved a consistently higher level of correlation between achievement and ability than had been indicated by student grades in previous years." If this finding was accurate, they would have good reason to claim that their English pilot program had very real merit.

Evaluating a Program for College Prep Students

Some say that minis are all right for non-academic students and for "fun" courses, but that they may not be appropriate for the college-bound. To test this, a highly academic high school in suburban New York did a systematic and thorough evaluation of their elective program. When it began, students were given a choice of taking either a traditional program or quarter electives. In the first year, two-thirds of the juniors and seniors, the classes eligible for the program, chose electives. The next year, three-fourths of the students did, and in the third year of the program only 15 percent of the students stayed with traditional courses. If one way to gauge the success of a program from a student's point of view is to see what happens to enrollments when students have a choice, this program could be judged a success.

Both parents and teachers wondered whether or not the elective students, with their often eclectic choices and frequent shifts of teachers, were learning to read and write as well as those in conventional courses. To assess this, the English department in cooperation with Educational Testing Service prepared an elaborate evaluation device which included both standard and special tests. Scores on these indicated that on the average students in both groups performed equally well on tests of basic skills. They also found that low-ability students in elective courses seemed to perform better on an achievement test than did their counterparts in the traditional course. If "holding its own" can be interpreted as a gain for an innovative program, this one was a success on another score.

This evaluation program also included subjective judgments from both teachers and students. Among the questions for students who had gone on to college was one on how they would compare their elective courses with the traditional courses they had taken earlier, and the response was that the students liked the electives better. The students also seemed to feel that the electives enabled them to make better connections between subject areas and to communicate more easily, both definite pluses. The students also felt that the teacher was the most important aspect of making a course good and that nine weeks were sufficient for teachers to judge a student's work fairly. In the end, the teachers felt that the elective program made the study of English more "palatable" and decided to adopt an all-elective program to replace the traditional one.

Integrating Evaluation with Development

Effective evaluation is an on-going process. Far too often those who do evaluate wait until the "end" and thus lose the guidance provided by an in-process appraisal. When a Nevada high school sought to develop an approach to make its curriculum more interesting and relevant, they decided to undertake a mini-class program and to include an on-going evaluation as an integral part of it. The first group of minicourses were semester-long ventures, to be evaluated at six-week intervals. The evaluation session at first was just an informal meeting between the administration and students and teachers. It revealed that the inadequate background of many students made their participation in classroom planning difficult. The administration also discovered that teachers who voiced initial opposition continued to resist the minicourse program and that the goals it had set for the minicourses were too broad. Knowing this at the beginning of the program enabled to school to modify the demands it placed on the students, to give the program more structure, and to let the non-enthusiastic teachers choose not to participate.

Theory Prods Practice

The opening sentence of this chapter calls attention to the fact that curriculum theorists stress the importance of building evaluation into curriculum improvement phases. Practice seems to be that, with few exceptions, evaluation seldom becomes an integral part of the change to minicourses. One explanation is that school people rarely appraise their traditional courses systematically, so why should they be expected to do so with short-term alternatives?

More fundamental is the failure to think through and clearly state the specific purposes of a curriculum innovation. Chapter two lists a number of high-sounding statements and goals for and about minicourses, but these are somewhat global in nature and do not easily lend themselves to evaluation. If a school does not clearly set out a plan for what students are supposed to accomplish as a result of a minicourse, how can it determine whether or not the efforts have been effective?

Thus, curriculum theory should be more than an abstraction. It should literally prod minicourse developers into: (1) examining their assumptions (students will do "better" if they have choices), (2) refining their objectives (students will gain a more positive attitude toward education), and (3) carefully setting up procedures that will provide information as to the strengths and weaknesses of the new courses.

Schools trying mini alternatives ought to attempt to get some kind of view of what is taking place, to note to what extent project goals are being attained, and to ascertain how participants feel about the new program. Many have taken these steps. The commonest method is to elicit student and teacher options through questionnaires and/or interviews. Another way to gather feedback is to have staff members pool their observations at department meetings. Some schools have made use of statistical data, especially on class enrollments, attendance records, and scores on standardized tests. Although minicourses are all relatively recent, only a few schools have conducted follow-up studies of graduates. Some schools have used external evaluation, either by calling in consultants or by reviewing the findings of an accreditation team.

What do these evaluation procedures seek to find? Some appraisal pictures are close-ups concentrating on one feature such as likes and dislikes or academic achievements. Other scenes are panoramic—taking a attitudes, achievement, discipline, teacher preferences, length of courses, frequency of offerings, parental perspectives, and planning procedures. The range of focus is from the merits of one course to the changing of the school year to year-round organization.

What does the evaluation picture reveal? In nearly every situation the bulk of the data supports the mini idea. Most of the students have been enthusiastic. Wherever negative statements have been made, they usually have touched on local conditions or specific dissatisfactions rather than being a rejection of the basic concept itself. Of great importance is the fact that the curriculum planners continue to make program adjustments in view of these appraisals. Evaluation improves decision-making.

"Overflow" Values

Although asking participants—by interview or by questionnaire—is a very common way to judge the acceptance of a program, there are other indices which may also serve as guides to the worth-whileness of a curriculum venture. These might be classified as serendipity—the faculty of making happy and unexpected discoveries. Others see results beyond the expected as having "overflow" values, fringe benefits that in the long run prove of great value.

Look at these actual statements from the field. From the mother of an elementary school boy: "When it's going to be minicourse day at school, my son is up early all ready to go to school long before school time." The program coordinator in that same school reports, "On minicourse day attendance is up. No one is going to the bathroom or to the drinking fountains. Maybe they are telling us something!"

The often stated goal of "student responsibility" is an intangible one, but there are reactions that give support to the contention that a minicourse program enhances the attainment of that goal. For example, teachers report that some of the self-direction associated with selecting and participating in minicourses carries over into conventional class situations. In free-form arrangements students often taken responsibility for working with younger student groups as well as for planning and leading sessions with their own classmates.

Very often analysis on curriculum innovations ends up with, "It's the teacher who makes the difference." Morton and Dei Dolori in talking about the electives approach declared, "We found improved morale between teachers and students, as both were involved in programs which best suited their abilities and interests. As a result there were considerably fewer student-teacher conflicts. Experienced teachers reported that discipline problems were greatly diminished due to the increase in student interest."*

---

*Thomas H. Morton and Mario P. Dei Dolori, "An Electives Program in a Small High School? It Works!" *English Journal* 60:952-56, October 1971.

Feelings affect learning. How students *feel* about their courses, about their teachers, about school in general, and particularly about themselves—all aspects of the affective domain—is increasingly being written about and discussed. While a learner may be able to regurgitate "correctly" a proof on congruent triangles (cognitive expectation), he or she may end up hating geometry (affective unexpected). The mini idea pressumably, with its emphasis on alternatives, gives students choices and flexibility. Filtering through the many feedback reports on experiences with minicourses are indications that feelings about courses, teachers, and selves are generally on the positive side.

Retrospect and Prospect

The atmosphere in education circles these days is charged with challenges. Some seem contradictory, or at least they are counterproductive. Among these challenges to curriculum makers are: options, basics, change, costs, individualized instruction, affective domain, differentiated curriculum, discipline, and indifferent attitudes.

These pages have attempted to survey the curriculum field with focus upon the phenomenon known as the minicourse. Contacts were made with schools across the country. The survey found that minicourses have appeared in many forms and with varying time plans. The essential features are: shorter than conventional courses that are based upon both teacher and student interest, courses that are elective, developed around stated objectives, and added or dropped as interest and demand decree. These elements are helping educators deal effectively with the challenges mentioned above.

With such potential it is not surprising that the minicourse "star" which appeared on the curriculum horizon in the 1960s has shone more brightly in the 1970s. There are cautions. There are problems—as in most innovations. However, the outlook for the 1980s will be a rewarding one for the curriculum stargazers.

An analysis of the underlying theory and the feedback from field operations indicates that the mini can become a curriculum maxi *if:*

— Arrangements are made that permit teachers to work with students in mutually satisfying and creative ways.
— The courses have a clear sense of purpose.
— The school really wants to individualize learning.
— Teachers and administrators are able to internalize the philosophy upon which the minicourse concept is based.
— Plans are made carefully and moves are made cautiously.
— There is movement.

References

Alonso, Elizabeth B., and Vega, Mirta R. "Quinmester Courses— What are They?" *American Foreign Language Teacher* 2:12-13 (Summer 1972).

Association for Supervision and Curriculum Development. *Evaluation as Feedback and Guide.* Washington, D.C.: By the Association, 1967.

Beckett, Dale. "Fairfield's Elective English: A Curriculum for Today to Meet the Needs of Tomorrow," *American Secondary Education* 1:36-40 (June 1971).

Bevan, John M. "The Interim Term: Its History and Modus Operandi," *The Library-College Journal* 2:20ff (Summer 1969).

Campbell, Lloyd P. "Humanizing School Through Minicourses," *Clearing House* 50:127-29 (November 1976).

Diamond, Edward. "Guidance at Long Beach High School: Quartered and Flourishing," *School Counselor* 23:51-53 (September 1975).

Farrell, Edmund. "English from Apex to Nadir: A Non-Elected, Omniphased, Opinionated, Untested Oral Examination of What's Up and Down," *The English Record,* October 1972.

Gorton, Richard A. "Student Reactions to the School Program," *NASSP Bulletin* 56:145-48 (September 1972).

Guaditis, Donald J. "Mini-courses: Are They Useful?" *Clearing House* 46:465-67 (April 1972).

Hillocks, George, Jr. *Alternatives in English: A Critique of Elective Programs.* Urbana: National Council of Teachers of English, 1972.

Kerr, William G. "A Study of Designated Affective Behaviors of High School Students Enrolled in Minicourses and Traditional Courses." Doctoral diss., Wayne State University, 1975.

Myers, Franklin G. "English Electives Passes a Test: An Abstract of an Evaluation of the Electives Program at Scarsdale High School," *The English Record* 21:52-60 (February 1971).

Nicholson, Everett. "Comments on Research: Student Uses of Unscheduled Time," *NASSP Bulletin* 57:105-8 (April 1973).

Oliver, Albert I. *Curriculum Improvement,* 2nd Ed. New York: Harper and Row, 1977. Ch. X "How May Curriculum Improvement Be Appraised?"

Paulson, James, et al. "The Unit Plan: The Promise of an Administrative Design," *Clearing House* 46:535-39 (May 1972).

Rossman, Jack E. "Student and Faculty Attitudes Toward the Interim Term: An Evaluation of Curriculum Innovation," *Liberal Education* 53:540-47 (December 1967).

Weise, Donald F. "Nongrading, Electing, and Phasing: Basics of Revolution for Relevance," *English Journal* 59:124-30 (January 1970).

Williams, George L. "English Electives Evaluated," *Clearing House* 47:469-71 (April 1973).

PARTICIPATING SCHOOLS

Some of the schools and school systems that participated in the survey upon which this book is based are listed below. Curriculum materials and other information provided by these schools were particularly useful in making this survey.

Alaska

Prince of Wales High School, Craig

California

Herbert Hoover High School, Fresno
Desert Sun School, Idyllwild
Katherine Delmar Burke School, San Francisco
Santa Barbara High School, Santa Barbara

Connecticut

Hamden High School, Hamden
Hall High School, West Hartford

Florida

Dade County Public Schools, Miami
Manatee County Public Schools, Bradenton

Georgia

Fulton County Public Schools, Atlanta

Hawaii

McKinley High School, Honolulu

Illinois

Romeoville High School, Romeoville
New Trier East High School, Winnetka

Indiana

Danville Community High School, Danville
Pike High School, Indanapolis
Shortridge High School, Indianapolis

Iowa

John F. Kennedy Senior High School, Cedar Rapids
Nodland Elementary School, Sioux City

Maryland

Walt Whitman High School, Bethesda

Massachusetts

Hamilton-Wenham Regional High School, Hamilton
Lexington High School, Lexington
Acton-Boxborough Regional High School, West Acton
Wilmington High School, Wilmington

Michigan

Trenton High School, Trenton

Minnesota

Pratt Elementary School, Minneapolis
St. Paul Open School, St. Paul

Missouri

Central Senior High School, Chesterfield
Logos School, St. Louis
McCluer North High School, Florissant
Sigel Elementary School, St. Louis

Montana

Bozeman Junior High School, Bozeman

Nebraska

Omaha Public Schools, Omaha

Nevada

Pershing County High School, Lovelock

New Hampshire

Lebanon Senior High School, Lebanon

New Jersey
>Deptford Township High School, Deptford
>Little Silver Elementary Schools, Little Silver
>North Hunterdon Regional High School, Annadale
>Rumson-Fair Haven Regional High School, Rumson

New Mexico
>Los Alamos, Los Alamos

New York
>John Dewey High School, Brooklyn
>Scarsdale High School, Scarsdale

Ohio
>Aurora Middle School, Aurora
>Fairview High School, Dayton
>Oberlin City Schools, Oberlin
>Carl F. Shuler Junior High School, Cleveland

Pennsylvania
>Bellefonte Area High School, Bellefonte
>Butler Area Junior and Senior High Schools, Butler
>Jersey Shore Senior High School, Jersey Shore
>Marple-Newtown High School, Newton Square
>Summit Elementary School, Wallingford
>Swissvale Area High School, Pittsburgh
>Wissahickon Senior High School, Ambler

Tennessee
>Chattanooga Public Schools, Chattanooga
>Memphis Public Schools, Memphis
>Nashville Public Schools, Nashville

Virginia
>Fairfax County Schools, Fairfax
>Hampton Public Schools, Hampton
>Maury High School, Norfolk
>Pimmit Hills Elementary School, Falls Church

Washington
>Stadium High School, Tacoma

Wisconsin
>Marshall Junior High School, Janesville